MYSTERIOUS
PLACES

*There is no terrain more obscure,
or revealing, than the past...*

*To the Millers
Warm regards
Jeffrey Gorney*

JEFFREY
GORNEY

Produced by:

FriesenPress

Suite 300 – 852 Fort Street
Victoria, BC, Canada V8W 1H8

www.friesenpress.com

Distributed to the trade by The Ingram Book Company

TABLE OF CONTENTS

In memory of my grandparents

who taught me not to be afraid of the dark

and my mother

who provided light.

PART ONE
THE STORIES

1
WHERE WE
CAME FROM

"Tell me about the Gypsies, Grandma..."

"The Gypsies?"

"When you were a little girl..."

"When I was a little girl in Romania," she began.

At bedtime, when I was a little boy, my grandmother would tell me her stories. Told and retold, each began the same way. "When I was a little girl in Romania" was Grandma's "once upon a time."

My grandmother could not read or write. Her voice was her pen, memories the color of her ink. By the light of my bedside lamp, she skillfully wove family fact into fable, unwittingly planting my soul in the Romania of her past. Here, in the dark, long gone voices spoke, faded fiddlers made music for the vanished dances of my grandmother's girlhood and the Gypsies came down from the hills.

"People were afraid they would steal children, but they never did," she said. "When the winter was over they came, the *Tziganes* , the Gypsies. They came into the town with their big copper pots, and they banged those pots with big copper spoons. We came out of our houses with our own pots, the ones we used for jam and food, the ones that got holes or got damaged during the year. The Gypsy men they repaired the pots.

"You should have seen them. They wore vests like the cowboys. And the women. What beauties. Hair black as night. Long braids they had, with shiny beads. Did I ever tell you about my hair? The color of wheat in the sun! Clara with the long gold braids. That's what they called me."

Grey was the color of my grandmother's hair. It was hard to think of her as ever having been blonde, no less young. Every morning she would come out of her bedroom, making her way to the kitchen in her nightgown with a single grey braid hanging down her back. She looked like Pocahontas, only old and from Europe. "My thin hair," she would say, pinning that braid back into a tight bun, time-honored insignia of the old women of East Flatbush, of whom there seemed to be legions. One by one, families had fled to an exotic place called "the suburbs," turning our neighborhood into a reservoir for grandparents.

The Italians, from what I had heard, came mostly from Sicily or Calabria, from towns and villages like Catanzaro and Cosenza or Aragona and Messina, names that tinkled on the tongue like chimes in the wind. The Jews, mostly from Russia or Poland, came from places that sounded as complex and eccentric as the traveled history of the Jews themselves. Minsk and Pinsk. Gdynia and Gdansk. Bialystoker, Kiev, and Warsaw. From regions they came that might as well have been make-believe. Silesia and Galicia. And Carpathia. Fairy tale kingdoms where, as it turned out, there would be no happy endings. Latvia and Lithuania.

Nobody, it seemed, came from Romania. Except for us, and no one knew what to make of us. We were neither Slavic nor genuinely Eastern European, as many thought. We were Balkan. We were Latinate. We were Judaic… and we were more.

Before Romania, there was Dacia where kings and noblemen reigned over soil so fertile and warriors so splendid that mighty Rome took note. It is said that among the Roman soldiers who came and conquered and Latinized, there were Jews. We were present at the creation.

We were there when the Turks swept up from the East to seize the land. Hundreds of years of Ottoman rule ended in a bloody war for independence but left an enduring legacy. Constantinople spiced future Romania's foods, domed its rooftops, and arched its doorways. We Romanians hung carpets on our walls, savored the aromatic buds of Turkish coffee, and elevated the baking of eggplant to an art form. Even Romanian, least known of the Romance languages and a gift of the Romans, would forever pulse with Turkish words and cadences.

Over the years before and after the Turks, others would raid this rich and beautiful country, from the Bulgars, Avars, and Mongols who helped forge Romanian identity, to the Soviets who suppressed it and, it has been said, ran off with the royal jewels.

We, the Jews of Romania, were there through it all. We even had our own unofficial anthem: *Romania Romania*, a cabaret tune of syrupy Yiddish lyrics and toe-tapping Romanian peasant verse. In our house, we listened to that old song on a scratchy 78, and our hearts sang…

O Romania, Romania, Romania, Ro-may-nya – Ro-may-nya
Was once a land, so sweet, and so fine there
What your heart desires, you can find there
A mamaliga, a pastrami
A carnati and a little glass of wine…

At bedtime, when I was a little boy, my grandmother would sing to me. Her voice was neither soothing nor sweet. Yet in songs molded of memory, it drew warmth from the house where she was born in the faraway village of Stefanesti. In Romanian, she sang of the flute player who made music out of tin and air. In Yiddish, she sang lullabies steeped in the nights of the distant East. To my dark room, her songs brought light and longing for all that was so well remembered...

I have for you a bride, is she a Romanian, nice figure.

She will cook for you a delicious mamaliga.

•   •   •

2
THE NEW WORLD

I am five, and I am standing on the stoop of our small apartment house next to my uncle Jack. His hair was rust-colored then, and Mommy said no man could be more handsome than her big brother.

"Jeffrey boy," my uncle said, "when I was a teenager, I used to ride my bike down here and there was nothing but those...." He points to the houses across the street. Old houses, one-family houses, grey houses, strung together like brick beads on a necklace. Nice houses with warm lights and window shades, except for one. A dark and empty house with a crack in the living room window, and a broken garden gate. A house where nobody had lived for a long time, maybe forever. Marsha and I call it the haunted house. We always run past it.

"When I was a boy," Uncle Jack said once more, "those houses stood alone. There was nothing else." He looked far away like he was somewhere else, maybe another time or another place. "Nothing," he repeated. "Not even sidewalks. Nothing but those houses, and fields."

I look at those houses as hard as I can. I try to see when Uncle Jack was a boy like me, and the houses were new and the grey bricks had not faded. Maybe someone lived in the haunted house then. Maybe there was a light on in the dark and you could hear someone playing a piano. I try to picture it. That long grey line of houses, all new and shiny, stranded in a field of grass.

On our side of the street half the block has houses that are newer, joined together two by two, like Siamese twins separated by driveways. Little red roses climb up out of little front gardens and onto little porches of orange, gold, and brown brick. You wouldn't think it was Brooklyn. We live down the block in the middle house of a trio of older boxy buildings, three stories each, squatting on the street like they were trying to keep the sidewalk from flying away.

Our building had "seen better days," Mom said. Well, its bricks are old and worn. Big iron lanterns on either side of the front door are always dark, and no one ever thinks to put in a bulb. Still it isn't so bad. Green hedges grow round a front garden where purple irises bloom in spring. I heard Uncle Louie say our house was built right before The Crash. Can you imagine such a thing? Maybe that's why everyone is waiting to move, wanting to live somewhere else—in case another Crash comes along.

I wonder if any of our neighbors appreciate the special things about our apartments. Kitchen cupboards reach way up to the ceiling. Fancy moldings pop out of the living room walls, and there's so much white tile in the kitchen that it's downright dazzling. Maybe the builders added these special touches because they knew The Crash was coming, or maybe it is because our part of East Flatbush is what Mommy calls "the better side of working class."

I am six and I remember the day. A spring day. Grandpa sits in one of the raspberry-colored chairs that guard the alcove in the living room. Dr. Mayseles hovers over him, peering through horn-rimmed glasses. "Mr. Cohen," he says, "if you do not eat, you will perish."

"I'll eat," Grandpa replies.

Smiling kindly, the doctor removes his cigar and exhales with a flourish. A plume of grey vapor wafts out of his mouth, proof of what I have always known: Dr. Mayseles is not only a genie possessed of undisputed wisdom, but also a demon that could turn the very air into mist. A hazy smoke ring floats lazily around Grandpa's unhappy face.

He coughs and nods toward the doctor, who smiles smugly and strides out of the house, confident as a magician.

Mayseles still has credibility with Grandpa, even after his ban on cigar smoking in effect since Grandpa's heart attack. I am too young to remember when it happened, but I know that cigars, now off limits, had been traditionally attached to Grandpa. I know this from one of my secret sources, hidden throughout our small apartment: the living room credenza. A snapshot, found in the forbidden top drawer shows Grandpa holding me on his knee, a well-dressed, bewildered boy of three. With his thick mustache, perfect posture, and high cheekbones, Grandpa looks like the Romanian soldier he once was.

Years later Uncle Jack would say to me: "You should have seen Grandpa in his heyday, Jeffrey boy, he looked like a matinee idol," whatever that was. The photo was snapped on the steps of the house where Uncle Jack and Aunt Ida live. On the flip side, I see a note that could only be called a powerful clue. Written in Mommy's handwriting, it reads: *Papa…What no cigar?*

Five years later the cigar wars still rage. "Mayseles says I shouldn't smoke," Grandpa grumbles. "And he sits there, with a big Havana in his mouth, huffing and puffing. Ha!"

Mayseles has been house doctor to the Vasluieur, which was an association for Romanian Jews. He had been their doctor for as long as anyone could remember, and for all of the carrying on, my grandparents think the world of him. To me, the sound of Vasluieur—*Vaz-lou-yah*—is pretty funny. My grandmother, in her broken English, calls my Uncle Louie "Lou-ya." So I figure the Vasluieur is named after him. Which says a lot about Louie since he isn't even Romanian.

The Vasluieur is what they call a fraternal lodge. I wonder and wonder what such a funny name like Vasluieur means and where it comes from. Mommy remembers going to meetings when she was a girl. Political and practical issues were debated, she tells me, with hotheaded fire. Fraternal brothers pounded on podiums, she recalls, while their wives nodded and clucked in support. Fingers wagged, voices rose, and creative curses flew across the hall. Over and over throughout the years, and with great joy, Grandpa would recall these.

"You should only get the Vasluieur hernia," yelled one angry member at another. "May you grow like an onion with your head in the ground," came the response.

Mom told me that Grandpa had been president. It is easy to see why, with his tall bearing and classy good looks. Though the Vasluieur meetings are way in the past, Grandpa still has an executive position: he takes care of arranging burials. Given the average age of the lodge members, the calls keep coming in and he is pretty busy and important.

I am unhappy today. It is Saturday and Mommy is going into work. She is an office manager for a place that manufactures fabrics for umbrellas. Can you imagine such a thing? It is a new job, and a step up from being a secretary. Mommy says she is going in on Saturdays so she can save money for me to go to college one day. Nobody in our family ever went to college before except cousin Norman, and he is a genius. Anyway I don't care about college. I care that Mommy works all week long, and most days she comes home from work just when I am going to bed. I hardly see her, so the weekends are very important to us. I hope this Saturday stuff is temporary.

The phone rings. Grandma picks it up. A Vasluieur member has just died, she says to Grandpa, her hand over the receiver. Aunt Betty, on one of her whirlwind visits, grabs the phone out of Grandma's hand. "I appreciate your calling," she says into the phone, a cigarette in her free hand, smoke swirling around her yellow hair and fair face. She is what Grandma calls natural platinum. "My father is getting on in years," my aunt goes on with regal authority. "He's not as young as he used to be. He's not always well. He can't handle this anymore." Betty slams the phone down, dispatching the caller, in her way.

I study her carefully. They say she looks just like Grandma when Grandma was young, blonde hair and all. They say that years ago a man followed Betty on the beach at Coney Island. She got real nervous until the man asked if her mother came from Iasi. The man had known Grandma in the Old Country, and he was sure that Betty had to be her daughter because they looked so much alike.

I can't see it. Grandma never wears lipstick or jewelry and her winter coats are hand-me-downs. Betty is always perfectly made up. She has red, red fingernails and red, red lips, and today she wears a leopard skin coat. Mommy says if her sister Betty wears leopard, you can bet your bottom dollar it is *real*. Imagine that. Aunt Betty wraps herself in the spotty fur of a real leopard and Uncle Louie drives a shiny black Cadillac. No wonder everyone in the family talks about how comfortable they are.

Mommy enters the room, looking sad.

Betty looks sternly at Mom, and then she shoots right up, tugs at the leopard and, shaking herself with a sense of royal right, starts to leave the room. She sure didn't act like a person who was comfortable.

Aunt Betty turns back and looks Mom in the eye. "What's wrong with *you?*" she snaps.

"Well, it's Saturday," Mommy answers. "I'm not so thrilled about going into work."

A shadow falls over Betty's pale face. You can see lines forming. Slowly and deliberately, and with an air of pained self-sacrifice, my mother's oldest sister spits out her response: "I suppose you think it's easy for me, getting in and out of the car all day."

• • •

3
TALES OF THE DRIVEWAY

Our small foyer, just off the kitchen, is my office. I sprawl across the blue lino-leum floor right next to the carved legs of the Brunswick radio. Ornate yet sinister to the eye, the Brunswick inspires fear in all who look at it. Big and old and dark, that Brunswick is a leftover from Grandma and Grandpa's life in the Bronx before us. My cousin Norman, much older than I, and already a promising physicist, eventually walked off with it. "I'm interested in the tubes," he announced. Grandpa thought that was pretty funny.

Anyway, it didn't matter to us. No one ever dared turn that big Brunswick on. We listen instead to the small wooden radio on top of the refrigerator. Everyone else on the block has televisions. I want a TV really badly, but Grandpa says that we are the smart ones. "We'll wait till they come out with color TV," he says.

In the olden days, when Mom was a girl, they didn't have a radio on top of the refrigerator. Come to think of it, they didn't have a radio anywhere because radio hadn't come out yet. They didn't even have refrigerators. Instead they had what was called an icebox to keep food and stuff cold. Imagine such a thing. On top of the icebox Grandma kept cups and saucers that came from England but were called China,

In London, Grandma's China had been proudly displayed in a breakfront, whatever that meant. In Brooklyn, she didn't have a breakfront so Grandma placed the cups and saucers on top of the icebox. In London she'd had three children. It Brooklyn she had five and they ran to the icebox a hundred times a day. They slammed that icebox door open and shut over and over, and one by one Grandma's delicate cups and saucers broke.

"What did I know?" Grandma would say, shrugging it off. But I think it mattered to her. She loved the life she and Grandpa lived in London, and we could all recite their address over there by heart: 45 Redmans Road.

It seems that every icebox had a man who came to fill it with ice in order for it to stay cold. Grandma's iceman was Dominic Scrafula who had come here from Italy. Dominic Scrafula's wife had just died and he was raising his two young daughters all by himself. Mom remembered watching Dominic Scrafula chop up the ice and put it in the icebox. When he finished, Grandma would serve tea. Then the two of them would sit for hours drinking tea, and Grandma would give Dominic Scrafula advice on bringing up children and keeping house.

"We had less in those days," I once heard Mom tell Uncle Jack, "but we were sweeter to each other." Uncle Jack wondered if people were that kind to each other anymore.

Dominic Scrafula must have meant a lot to Grandma because she held onto his ice pick for years. It was still in a drawer in the kitchen cupboard, along with Grandpa's cooper's tools.

Grandpa sits now at the little table in the corner of the kitchen, next to the big maple table. He is playing pinochle with an imaginary partner. He has taught Grandma how to play, but she is usually too busy. Snaring a real live partner is always a victory for Grandpa.

"Mrs. Cohen!"

The voice belongs to Aunt Henny. She yodels from her kitchen window to ours, across the driveway that separates our house from its red brick twin. Henny is not really my aunt. She is more like a second mother to me. Her daughter Marsha is my girlfriend. Her husband, Uncle Nat delivers fruit to the local groceries. We go everywhere in Uncle Nat's truck. Smelling of fresh lettuce or ripe peaches, we go to the movies, to visit Aunt Henny's friends, or to see her father in what appears to me to be a shadowy apartment in Williamsburg, the old neighborhood where all the grownups grew up.

"Mrs. Cohen!!!!"

"Henicu!" Grandma answers, opening our window with one hand, a big kitchen knife held firmly in the other. "Cu" in Romanian means "dear little one" when attached to the end of a name. Mom is *Eticu*. Cousin Sylvia is *Sylvacu*. My great-aunt Rae calls me, of all things, *darlingcu*. "Cu" is a sign of great affection. Aunt Henny is American born. Her husband and parents are from Russia. What, I wonder, does she thinks Henicu means.

"You remember my cousin Luba, Mrs. Cohen?"

"The nervous one?" Grandma asks. "The one who paints pictures?"

Henny nods "yes." Then a deep breath. "She snapped, Mrs. Cohen."

"Snapped?" Grandma asks, not quite understanding.

Aunt Henny twirls her index finger to her head to signify madness.

"You mean…?" Grandma said, putting the big knife down, and twirling a finger to her own head.

"Yes, Mrs. Cohen. She's mental!"

Grandma picks up the big knife and points it to the heavens, a grand gesture reserved for unexpected and great tragedy. "Oh," she moans, looking for all the world like the matriarch in a stormy Greek drama. "So young, so pretty."

"A little on the chunky side," Aunt Henny said. "But a pretty face, and what a talent! When she painted an apple or a strawberry, you looked at it, you could taste it." Aunt Henny thinks for a minute.

"They're always the first to go, the talented ones," she says. Then she is quiet, as if to let her words sink in, followed by an abrupt, customary change of pace. "Listen, Mrs. Cohen. Take Jeffrey to the Rugby. A picture you'll enjoy. Color. Music. An actress you'll love. Ann Blyth. A face like an angel, and she sings too."

"Ann *Blight*," Grandma repeats. Over the years, in her broken English, my grandmother had rechristened an honor roll of movie stars with fractured versions of their glamorous names. Uncle Louie loved to tell, how in the days of the silents, Grandma turned screen siren Clara Bow into Clara Boat. Mommy remembers that when she was a girl, Grandma changed William Powell to William Towel. In my time, Marilyn Monroe became Marilyn Magrum. "Ann Blight," Grandma said aloud slowly to ensure proper pronunciation.

"So I hear you have a guest today," Aunt Henny said, changing the subject again.

"Yes," Grandma replied, nodding in silent acknowledgment.

"I wonder how she'll look to you, that Jenny, after all this time, Mrs. Cohen."

"Don't worry, Henny. She'll look fine, and she'll be fine. Like we used to say in the Old Country: The greedy pig always gets the apple that falls nearest the tree."

• • •

4

AN EXOTIC VISITOR

I open my trusty *World Book Encyclopedia* to a page of colorful maps. Reading by the slice of light that spills in from our white-tiled kitchen, I stare at bold black letters that read R-O-M--R-U-S: code for Romania-Russia. My eyes wander all over the secret map.

Grandpa sits at his little table in the corner, next to the big maple table. Forsaking pinochle for the newspaper, he reads aloud, "Rock n' Roll is a curse," he says, in that British way he has of speaking. "Rock 'n roll is responsible for … *juvenile delin-quency.*" His voice thunders across the kitchen and he shakes a finger at me. "Watch yourself!" he says.

Grandma unwraps a pale green box with cake fresh from the bakery. My father's mother, Grandma Jenny, is coming to visit. We have not heard a word from my father since he vanished. That was a couple of years back. I don't remember it, but I found out what happened.

One night there was a big storm and all the lights blew out. The whole house was dark, except for the kitchen. I crept out of my bedroom, running on tiptoes across the dangerously dark living room to hide behind the monstrous Brunswick, near the kitchen entrance.

Rain pounded the windows. Candlelight flickered on the shiny white kitchen doorway. I could hear whispers. Grandma and Grandpa and Mommy were sitting around the big, maple table. I had to lean in and listen hard to hear them. I knew they were talking about my father.

"What kind of a man leaves his wife and child?" Grandpa said. "Whoever heard of such a thing? Taking out the garbage at night and never coming back!"

"You'd think somebody from the family would have been in touch all this time," said Mom.

"Usually," said Grandma, "in a case like that, the grandma would be the one. She is the one to smooth things over."

"Jenny!" Grandpa snorted. "She is something, that woman."

She must have been *something*. When I was bad they would say: "We'll send you to Grandma Jenny!" as if nothing could be worse, not even what my grandfather called "reform school," the building, he said, with walls of concrete nine-feet high and barbed wire. I don't take it seriously. I am excited to have a grandmother I have never seen, no less one who is "something."

Mom told me that Jenny and my other grandfather had lived in London, just like the grandparents who raised me. My other grandfather had been a sculptor. He was the nice one, she had been told. But he died young and suddenly, leaving Jenny alone in London with five little sons. "She never let you forget how she suffered," Mommy said, with a sour note in her voice.

Jenny had sent her oldest boy, Uncle Jerry, back to Poland to live with his grandparents. The others she took with her to America, my father being the youngest.

The Gorneys became fabled. They lived for me in snapshots, stories, and questions sometimes unanswered.

"What did Jenny do?" I asked.

"She was a corsetiere," Mommy said. "She made corsets for big shot ladies, even silent screen actresses, and she did okay for herself. She was what you call 'shrewd.'"

"She was a tough cookie," Grandpa added. "When she went to the movies, Jeffrey, she always sat with a hatpin in her hand."

"In case someone got fresh," Grandma said, rolling her eyes.

I am looking at the map. Jenny's Poland is too far from Romania to fit on the ROM-RUS page. Grandpa says Romania is "Behind the Iron Curtain." Can you imagine such a thing. An entire country separated from the rest of the world by a curtain made of iron! Everyone talks about the Iron Curtain, yet I can't find it anywhere on this map. Maybe it is the black line that separates Romania from Russia. Maybe that is why the black line is so thick.

On the map, Romania is an oddly shaped magenta mountain squatting on top of a pale blue pillow called Bulgaria. For a country behind an iron curtain Romania is kind of pink and pretty and doesn't look so bad.

Russia, to the right and flame colored, looks like the red skies of a forest fire, so big it could swallow Romania whole. Within the borders of red Russia, faint grey letters spell out the word *Ukraine,* and under it, *Moldova…*

There, just across the river from Iasi—where Grandma lived—lay the city of Kishinev, where Grandpa was born and raised. Grandpa says Kishinev, which is now Chisinau was in Bessarabia, a place that has somehow, magically, turned into Moldova. In his time it went back and forth between Bessarabia, which was then in Russia, and Romania. He told me that he even served in both armies. He made it very clear that he considered himself a Romanian.

Grandpa shuffles his pinochle deck. Calm settles over the kitchen. The clock ticks. Music from Mr. Nalibov's radio, across the driveway, drifts in through the window. All is still as we wait for our honored guest. Grandma places the freshly sliced cake on a platter.

A sudden shriek barrels through plaster and wood, piercing our kitchen ceiling from the kitchen above. Grandma nearly drops the cake dish. It's Irene Axelrod upstairs, on the warpath again. "Susan Rita!" she yells. "Drink the milk!"

A scuffling of feet follows. Grandma, still clutching the platter, looks up from the kitchen counter. Grandpa flips a playing card; he could care less. I look into the kitchen from my office on the foyer floor. Staring at the ceiling, I can just see my friend Susan Rita, skinny as a broomstick, Band-Aids over the scabs on her knees, and running like crazy across the kitchen upstairs.

See the pyramids along the Nile...

A woman's voice, smooth as honey, glides into our kitchen, direct from Nalibov's radio across the alley.

I am back on the map, this time exploring a fearful country to the left of Romania: a big silver knife of a place where people are commanded into slavery. The name tells all. You – Go – Slavia.

More scuffling upstairs. "Susan Rita, you spill that milk down the drain again, I'll kill you."

Watch the sunrise on a tropic isle....

Just remember darling all the while ...

Yugoslavia has even more names in pale print than giant Russia. These are weird little places that all end in the letter "a": Slovenia, Croatia, and Bosnia and Herzegovina. These last two I know from my stamp book are countries where stony-faced men with thick mustaches look at you sternly from under spiked helmets.

You belong to me

Da-da-da-dahhhh!

While the radio lady keeps on singing, my finger continues tracing a line from one "a" place to another till I get to Serbia. Of all the "a" places in Yugoslavia, tiny Serbia sits closest to Romania, separated from it by a curvy blue line of a river called the Danube. Right on top of Serbia and to the upper left of Romania lies the big gold platter of Hungary.

A door opens upstairs. Leo Axelrod is home.

"Daddy. She hates me!" Sue cries.

"You see, you see, Leo?" Irene shouts. "You see what I have here!"

Fly the ocean in a silver plane...

All of a sudden the song about looking at rivers and flying over oceans stops. The Nalibovs have turned off their radio. I can just see them. Irving with his sweet, sad, lined face and Lena with her fiery red hair and wide nostrils. "Like the Mississippi River," Grandpa had said. Aunt Henny told Mommy she'd seen Lena in the beauty parlor, and her red hair was white as snow. I am certain the Nalibovs turned off their radio on purpose, so they could listen to the Axelrods across the alley.

"Drink the milk," Leo says soothingly.

"Milk makes me puke."

"You're not here with her all day," Irene whines, on the brink of tears. "You don't know what I go through, Leo. God give me strength, what am I raising, a child or an animal!"

"Calm down," Leo says. "Everyone, calm down."

"I hate milk!"

"Drink your milk, Sue. Children are starving in Europe."

"Oh, Daddy, you're so stupid."

Grandma looks up at the ceiling. "Some way to talk to the *tata*," she said, using the Romanian. Shifting her glance to Grandpa, she sighs. "Jenny will be here soon."

Grandpa rises and heads for the foyer.

A moment later he appears in the kitchen doorway, wearing his big herringbone tweed overcoat. He puts on his cap. It looks like the cap that newsboys wear in the old movies. But Grandpa was never a newsboy; he was a cooper, or barrel maker, so I figure it is a cooper's cap.

"What are you doing, Aba?" Grandma says. "Where are you going? Jenny will be here any minute."

"I'm going out into the world. I can't stand to look at her. I can't stand her Polish face."

He did the same thing, I am told, when my father came to visit me a few years earlier. "If I have to look at him," Grandpa had said, "I'm afraid of what I'll do."

That visit was legendary. I was three. My father had joined the Navy after leaving us, and I can see him and a buddy of his sitting at the kitchen table in their navy blue sailor suits. I don't know if I really remember it or if it was spoken of so often that I think I remember it. But I do recall something that no one could have told me.

I am very little. I see in front of me a green glass bowl filled with apples on the kitchen table. My grandmother has just placed it there. The Navy buddy reaches for an apple. He looks at me.

"Pretty little boy," he says.

"He has a pretty mother," says my father.

A week or two later, I receive my first picture postcard ever. It is from my father, and it shows a cartoon figure of a fat sailor sitting on a rickety bench. Under his big rear end, lively letters spell out: "The Navy's in great shape." I roll on the floor. I am laughing so hard I think my sides will split.

Then I see something. On the upper left side of the card, in really nice handwriting, my father has written the word: "Forget..."

On the upper right corner: "Me."

On the lower left: "Not."

"Forget me not."

In the final corner, he writes, simply: *Daddy.*

• • •

5
OUR NEW LIFE

First my mother called the local hospitals, then the police. With no word of my father anywhere, she turned to a girlhood friend who lived down the block, and together they set out to find him. They checked in with my father's brothers. They went to his gym, to the office where he worked, and to places where he hung out. No one had seen him. No one knew anything.

Passover fell that week, and our family was set to gather at Grandma and Grandpa's house for the Seder, a traditional feast ironically celebrating Jewish escape from ancient bondage. For my mother and me, it was the beginning of what could well have been the opposite. For her it meant facing the entire family in a moment that would define the meaning of "public failure."

It would also unleash a flood of familial devotion that was Biblical in magnitude. Our family protected us with armor hammered out of centuries of collective calamity steeped in the harsh and volatile reality of a nomadic heritage. They wrapped us in a cocoon that warmed us, kept us safe from harm, and allowed us to flourish in fearful and untried territory.

Everyone pitched in. Aunt Ida's sister had found an apartment for herself and her young family but turned it over to us. Grandma and Grandpa were imported from the Bronx to run the house while my mother worked, and to keep us going. Uncle Louie had supported them ever since Grandpa retired, and he would continue to pay the rent.

My father never came around. There were no letters, no more funny postcards, or birthday cards. You would have thought telephones had not been invented yet. Financial support from him was minimal, and an amount he elected to pay. Even as my father shook the family tree, he changed the landscape of our lives.

"In those days most women stayed home," Mom recalled. "I never thought I'd go back to work again."

But she did and the way that she did it said lots. She never blackened my father's name. She never complained. If my father ducked out the back door into darkness, my mother walked out the front, head held high, into the blaze of a new and uncertain day. Like a pioneer woman facing wilderness, she marched proudly in the front lines of the first brigade of working mothers. She made more than the most of it, and was I proud.

She was not like the others. We were not so much different as distinguished by circumstance. My friends' mothers ruled worlds that smelled of Ajax and paste wax. Baggy housedresses were their uniforms, and dust rags and mops their ammunition. I watched them work hard, cleaning small apartments or little houses till windows sparkled like mirrors and you could eat off the floors. I also heard them come to life on the phone, gabbing about games with strange names like Canasta and Mah Jongg. I caught them snuggling into puffy armchairs, a smoky cigarette in one hand and paperback book in the other, all the while keeping an eye on us kids.

My mother went another route. Looking like she could buy the world, she left the house early each morning to work in that glamorous city across the river that we called "New York."

Living in the bowels of Brooklyn, you might as well have been in the Midwest. Most of our neighbors went into "the city" once in a very long while just to see the hit Broadway show or the big movie. Most of my friends spent Saturdays playing stoopball, hanging out on the corner, or at the movies. I went into Manhattan with my Mom. She took me to Broadway shows, to city events, and to museums. We went on vacations.

All that shaped me, and it shaped her. She became more than she would have been. She acquired a degree of sophistication. She became, in a small way, a Manhattan career woman. My mother had placed a sunny spin on a potentially gloomy situation. Best yet, she did it with a smile. But she didn't do it alone.

Grandma ran the house, cooked, cleaned, and took me to school. Grandpa took me to the barber, told me his stories, dispensed advice, and became my confidante. It was as if my grandparents were my parents and my mother was my older sister. We were an unconventional but happy household, and we were central to an imperiled species: the tightly knit and very loyal extended family.

Outside of my aunt and uncle in California, everybody lived within walking distance of our place, and they all visited Grandma and Grandpa on Sunday. During the week, my grandfather's nephews came to do repairs, and nieces came to say hello. Aunts and their lady friends came to offer moral support and gossip with Grandma. They all doted on me.

An elaborate network of obscure relatives paraded also through our door, at best to pay homage to my grandparents who were matriarch and patriarch of the family and at the very least to supply Grandpa with breathing pinochle partners.

Yet for all the affection and attention showered upon me, unseen ghosts emerged with unexpected and unsettling power. Running into the hallway foyer of our small building, I would see six mailboxes in a row. These were the families who lived in our house, our neighbors, and our friends. This was our village. Glimpsing the nameplates as I ran by, ours never failed to jump out at me and slap me in the face. Cohen-Gorney, it read, and there was more to that than met the eye.

We were different, Cohen-Gorney said to me, and to everyone else who saw it. We were a hyphenated family. As happy as we seemed to be, and were, my mother and I did not have our own sovereignty. We were stuck on, attached not just to my grandparents, but also to Uncle Louie and Aunt Betty, who paid the rent. There was something else, something not quite formed in my mind, but always there, simmering, waiting to surface.

My grandparents created such a buffer against unhappiness that, in those early years, my father's absence seemed not to matter. When I thought about him, I wondered where he was, and did he think about me. Deep down inside, I asked myself: would our lives somehow be better if he were around? Would we be just like everyone else?

"What does your Daddy do?" was a constant schoolyard challenge, and the answer determined where you stood among your pals.

"I don't know," came my response.

This, in an era when broken families and single parents were the exception, was met with vacant stares or curious questions that demanded careful clarification.

"My parents are divorced, and my father doesn't live with us," I would say,

Patiently and repeatedly I explained the situation, and a diplomat was born. No matter how you viewed it and no matter how warm and secure the home I grew up in, mine was an uncommon existence. Years later, in the heat of analysis, I would find that my father's absence was the most profound loss possible. Most boys think their dads run the world and own the moon. Father's are powerful.

There was something else. "You've got the pretty mother," my friends on the block would say. True, Mom was attractive and chic, but for me it went beyond that. My mother was American-born and she spoke perfect English. She was my credential. The problem was that none of my schoolmates really knew her. They knew Grandma.

It was Grandma who took me to school when I was younger and who carried out the duties of a mother. She was only 65 when she began to raise me. But being in your sixties in her time was not what it is now, and being European meant coming from another world. Sixty-five and European then meant that my grandmother wore the uniform of an ancient and foreign-born lady and she spoke funny. Kerchiefs perpetually framed her lined face. She wore coats that were cast offs from her daughters and daughters-in-law, and shoes made to support feet that had walked long and hard on this earth.

There was a trade-off that escaped me as a boy. In that time, on the heels of unprecedented war and economic disaster, yet in a world still connected to its past, age demanded respect. My teachers, all women and mostly young, confided in Grandma and sought her advice on family and personal matters. Only Grandma knew that my kindergarten teacher was pregnant; that my first grade teacher's daughter was about to marry another teacher's son, and how should they plan the wedding; that one teacher needed advice on how to handle an errant husband; and another on how to set up a new household. Grandma was a saint to these women, but to me her age and old-fashioned ways were unavoidable signage of how different we were.

"Please," I would beg her, "wear lipstick so they'll think you're my mother." She asked help of a neighbor lady who, rising to the occasion, painted pink lipstick on Grandma's old lips, powdered her worn face, and placed a tortoise comb in the knot of her silver hair.

• • •

6

FOOTSTEPS IN
THE DARK

There is nothing more rewarding to me than the sound of footsteps coming down the tile floor of the building hallway. A mild shuffle means Grandpa. The clickety-clack of high heels means Mommy is back from work. The turn of the doorknob is a sound of joy. She's home.

Clickety-clack. High heels. But Mom is already home. These are the footsteps of a stranger. High heels that stop suspiciously at the cellar door. Everyone coming to our house hurries past the door to the cellar, which is right next to our front door. It is always dark in the hall. No one ever opens the cellar door. It is an unknown place to be avoided at all cost. It is a place of dread mystery, and only a fool would linger there.

The outdoor cellar entrance, to the left of the stoop steps, is just as frightening, even in daylight. No one ever speaks about the basement to our apartment house. They say that the landlords, Mr. and Mrs. Horowitz, once rented it to a young men's club. But that was a long time ago.

Grandpa and Mr. Horowitz didn't get along. Horowitz ran the house on a shoestring. Heat was doled out as if it was gold and in winter Grandpa said our apartment was like Russia. One icy day when I was a baby, or at least too young to remember, my mother knocked on the landlord's door.

"It's very cold in our apartment," she said. "Could you turn up the heat?"

"Wear a sweater," he answered.

After hearing about that one, my grandfather never spoke to Mr. Horowitz again.

A few years later, when I was five or six, I had already developed the habit of running up the front stairs at record speeds, and for good reason. Fear ruled my life then. Some might call it blind fear but it is more than even that. I call it the nameless dread—and it is spurred by not knowing exactly what, or who, lurked behind that outside cellar door. This is a door that was never opened, always locked, and never mentioned. That outside cellar door is almost as frightening as the inside door right next to our apartment. It takes me a long time to figure out the secret behind the cellar door. One word said it all: Nazis!

Everyone is still talking about those Nazis and I figured it out. That's where they were, still hanging around and doing their evil deeds even though The War, as people called it, has been over for five or six years. God knows what those Nazis are up to now, or what they might have in store for a boy like me.

It was a stormy day when the terrible event happened. It was a day so cloudy and so dark that you could sense, you could absolutely feel, those Nazis stirring, up to no good in the basement. That's when it happened. That's when I heard, for the first time ever, a strange noise from behind the cellar door.

Well, it wasn't exactly a noise but a squeak of something turning slowly. This is the dirty work of a masked stranger, hand gloved in leather, fingers tightening around the cellar doorknob, rotating it, gaining entry to the world outside, to the front of the house where I stand alone. This is the iron fist of a Nazi.

Sprinting up the stoop stairs as fast as I can, I push in the front door, the weight and majesty of its iron scrollwork no match for the frenzy that drives me. Lickety-split I run through the little foyer, past those telltale mailboxes to the inner door with its hundreds of little windowpanes. I reach for the doorknob so quickly that I miss it and my fist sails right through one of the panes. Glass flies. Wood splinters. I run like crazy down the dark hall. Chips and slivers of glass, downright daggers, crunch under my feet.

I zoom past Horowitz's apartment, then the inside cellar door. Home at last I slam our apartment door behind me. That is when I hear Horowitz, in the hall, yelling at the top of his lungs.

"Who's there? What happened?"

A few days later he died, they said of a heart attack. Whenever news came that someone had died, Grandma would let go with this standard speech of hers, glorifying the deceased.

"So young," she cried. "Leaving a widow, oh my God, and two nice young sons."

"He was a son of a bitch when he lived," said Grandpa. "And he's still a son of a bitch!"

I am sure it is my fault that Mr. Horowitz died suddenly and too young, succumbing to shock inflicted by unexplained shattered glass in the foyer doorway. I lay low sweating bullets, waiting for disaster to take me. A week goes by, then two. ...

A knock. Grandma opens our door. A single clickety-clack indicates the visitor has entered. I am playing on the floor of the living room, just off the foyer. I look up. Two sets of shoes face each other. Grandma's shoes are black old lady shoes with firm laces. The other pair of shoes is high-heeled, the very same high heels that dared to stop in front of the cellar door. High heels of navy blue.

The two women look at each other for a moment. "Come on in, Jenny," Grandma says.

Grandma Jenny! I know grandmas. I live in a neighborhood that is filled with them. Grandmas don't wear high heels. Or lipstick. Grandmas are old ladies who stare out of windows and sweep stoop steps or, if they are lucky, dote on old men who sit on porches, reading their papers or gazing at forgotten dreams trapped in treetops. "Grandpa! Grandma!" you would hear kids call as they came to visit on Sundays. Grandpas wore suspenders and starched white shirts. Grandmas wore dark old lady dresses and hair in a braid that crowned the head or pinned back in a bun, like my grandmother.

Jenny Gorney is no ordinary grandma. There she stands, fine and straight, "like a statue of liberty," my other grandmother would later say. On the lapel of Jenny's trim grey suit, a silver pin glistens. Her white hair curves up in a fashionable pompadour. Silver earrings shaped like leaves dangle from her ears. She looks at me for what seems like a long time, not moving. Then she hands me a paper bag. I eagerly unwrap it to find a glass airplane filled with little colored beads.

Jenny's cherry red lips form a tight smile. "They're candies, Jeffrey," she said.

I turn the plane this way and that. I couldn't figure out how to get the candies out of the plane without breaking the glass.

"You look well, Ethel," I hear Jenny say to my mother.

"You, too," said Mom. "That's a nice suit."

"Well," Jenny said, tugging the sides of her smart suit. "I may be retired but I have people to see. I have to go to the bank after all. I was in business. I was a business-woman, not a scullery maid."

A long chilly silence follows. Then they talk and stop and talk again, but I no longer listen. My mind tackles the problem at hand. Herbie Breslin and the Bad Boys—this gang around the corner—they would know how to open the glass plane, get the candy out, and glue the plane back together again. And you'd never know it'd been cracked open.

Marsha and I never play with the Bad Boys. They are a wild bunch, but they always help out when you have a tough problem, like this.

No one is talking anymore. I glance up. Jenny is looking at me. She smiles. She beams. She never kisses me.

Grandma and Mommy are looking at Jenny, too, but she never looks back at them. Suddenly her eyes dart across the room and land on a forgotten part of the kitchen: a small canyon carved into the wall under the kitchen window, a place of secrets.

Grandma calls it *the Luche*. It has a little white enamel cover with a knob, and when you pull it the small door opens slowly. Translated from the Yiddish, *the Luche* means "the hole." I know its real meaning. This is no hole; this is a dungeon.

The Luche had been dug out of the wall. It is a cavern recessed so deep under the windowsill that it reaches the outside brick. To place one's hand in *the Luche* is to know cold. No matter how the radiator in the kitchen sputters, no matter how steamy the room, *the Luche* remains as cool as the frost that fogs our windowpanes in the dead of winter.

When no one is around, I pull the knob of *the Luche* open…and dare to peer inside. Within its icy heart, a strange garden grows. To one side lay onions huddled in a net bag, pearly skins shimmering in the shadows. Soon thick green vines will begin to sprout from the shiny peels, pushing against the small door, yearning to reach out. In back of the onions, I see a sack of potatoes, dusty brown hides sprouting ugly warts.

In the very front of the opening there rests a bunch of crimson beets topped by crude coffee-colored stems. Propped against the back wall, behind the beets and the potatoes and the onions, I can make out the gilded neck of a bottle of champagne. Where it came from and why it would be housed in a dark home for roots and growths is beyond me. Grandpa said we would open the bottle when Mommy got married again. On my sixteenth birthday, we threw the champagne out. The next year my mother remarried.

Time has come to a standstill. Jenny keeps staring at *the Luche*. Mommy and Grandma stay silent. I know the truth! This is no ordinary grandma. This is a high-heeled lady of mystery. This is a woman who had dared to stop at the cellar door when others scurried by in blind fear. This is my fabled Grandma Jenny, a stranger in our kitchen, casting a knowing glance at *the Luche*.

Jenny looks at me. We lock eyes. Her left eyebrow, finely lined with mascara, lifts, and she smiles. This time, an odd half-smile out of the corner of her mouth…a smile that says: "I know the truth. I know what festers in that sad little hole under the shiny white sill of your kitchen window, young Jeffrey. Don't think you can fool Grandma Jenny. I know where potatoes turn nasty and onions hide champagne."

Yes, she knows what others do not know, and so do I. How could a grandmother, so long unseen, become suddenly visible? How could a stranger know the secret of the dungeon? There is only one answer. Jenny is a witch. I had heard her called that before.

• • •

7

SECOND CHANCE

There are no other Gorneys on earth beside my mother and me, or so I believe. In a funny kind of way I think that I am special. No one else has my last name. There are no classmates, neighbors, or anyone named Gorney. No one is like me.

My father and the other Gorneys—his Gorneys, those Gorneys, the Gorneys that I come from—are a strange lot. They are half of me, I guess; the part of me that I belong to but do not know.

My father lives for me in the return address on the support checks that come from the County Courthouse, in a handful of photos leftover from his life with my mother, and for a while, with me. The most treasured is a novelty souvenir from their wedding, a pocket mirror with their portrait on the flip side. There they are, my folks, staring right at me: he in a snazzy tux, she in a beautiful white satin gown. How proud and happy they look.

Daydreams dance about in my little world, gauzy make-believe moments that magically bring him back to us. With a look of joyous triumph he stands, a hero at our foyer door, on the threshold of our lives. Always he wears his Navy pea coat, sailor cap in place, and a warm smile on his face. Always my mother enters the foyer in her wedding dress. Looking just like her exquisite pocket mirror self, she sails through the small foyer and into my father's waiting arms.

That great boyhood fantasy, born of natural yearning, will fall prey to the passage of time. Eventually it will evaporate, even as clues to my father's mysterious actual being slowly emerge.

We know that he is remarried. We know he lives in Westchester. Somehow we know that he has other children. However the Gorney family, and the name itself, remain an unexplained presence hovering on the edge of reality, a phantom of the heart.

Time would reveal that Gorney is not as uncommon a name as I had thought, surfacing often in areas with substantial Polish communities. Yet where I grew up, it lingered in a lonely place, and I knew deep down inside, on some unspoken level, that our seemingly rare last name will one day lead me to my father.

It would come on the heels of coincidence and without expectation, as important moments often do. This time the crucial event is as irrelevant—and ironic—as learning a new language, but a lot easier.

A forthcoming vacation in France prompts me to take a crash course in French. During that class, I befriend a fetchingly vibrant young woman who might as well have been a stylish young heiress, the breezy heroine of one of those classic screwball comedies. Auburn-haired and perfectly made up, she dresses with sass that suits her personality and she works, appropriately, in the fashion industry.

Class breaks soon become "our" time and one night, over a steaming cup of hot chocolate, my lively new friend asks what, under ordinary circumstances, would have been a question of no consequence.

"I've been wondering," she says, "are you related to Janice Gorney?"

"She's a first cousin," I answer. "But she won't know who I am."

I explain the situation and can't help but smile. I sense what is going to happen. Sure enough, the following week my French-school friend tells me she'd spoken to Janice and the news is surprising. Janice knows our story. As she is a few years older than I, she was very young but nonetheless around when it happened, and she even has vague memories of my mother. My newfound friend would become the go-between and the bearer of news that I know to be inevitable: my newfound cousin wants to meet me.

One week later, I appear at Janice Gorney's place in what seems like the ninetieth floor of a super duper Art Deco high-rise overlooking Central Park. I walk into a rambling 1930s apartment with spacious rooms that barely wrapped around massive pieces of tufted, overstuffed, and no-nonsense furniture. Lots of dark leather.

In the doorway, warm and welcoming, stands my cousin Janice, a handsome woman with a mane of blonde hair, and an easy smile sparked by my blue eyes and my high cheekbones. I had never really looked like anyone else before.

"You're a Gorney," Janice said, pointing to "our" telltale eyes and cheekbones. "*She* gave them to us."

"You mean Jenny?"

"Yes."

We talk, and I eagerly consume everything and anything I could glean about my father, his "second" family, and the other long-lost Gorneys.

As we rehash the past, I parrot what I'd overheard years back: that usually in this kind of situation, it was "the grandmother who would smooth things over."

Janice laughed. "Jenny? You don't know who you're talking about. She's the Wicked Witch of the West."

We talk and talk and talk some more. Finally I hear what I fully expect to hear, what I absolutely want to hear, what I always knew I would hear.

"Your father knows you're here, and he wants to meet you."

"Tell my father I want to meet him. Tell him not to be shy about being in touch."

As the afternoon passes, Janice reveals that my mother and I had evolved into a well-kept secret, never mentioned by my father, never referred to by the family, or by his second wife. That said a lot, but I did not realize it. All I could think is how all that had suddenly changed. But there was more.

Janice's Dad owned a store. The two brothers were close and my father had paid a usual visit just the other week. They were talking, and out of the blue, my uncle broke 28 years of silence with a real zinger: "Janice knows someone who knows Jeffrey."

My father burst into tears.

Did he think about me?

It's all right, I say to myself, he thought about me. He remembered.

"Tell my father to call me," I reiterated.

From that moment on panic filled the air. Two weeks went by, time mired in molasses, and nothing happened. I was certain my father had forgotten me yet again.

Finally, one sunny afternoon, the phone rang, with that kind of ring that you know means this is no ordinary call.

• • •

8
GUEST APPEARANCE

I remember your Uncle Jack," said the voice on the other side of the phone, the voice of a stranger. "What a nice man, and as nice as he was, that's how nice his wife was."

The voice belongs to Janice's father, my long-lost Uncle Harry Gorney, who explained he was calling on behalf of my father to make sure that I really wanted to meet him.

A visual memory flashed to mind. I see my sailor father sitting in our kitchen with his Navy pal. Then comes a vocal memory. I can hear my mother talking about a letter she'd received from another, or perhaps the same, Navy buddy. He was writing on behalf of my father to convey feelings of remorse and a plea to be taken back. It is not lost on me that my father again corralled a friend into intervening on his behalf. It seems he always needed a safety net, an assistant person, someone to speak up for him. "I didn't want him back," my mother said. "But if he wanted to come back, the way to have done it was through you. I thought we would always be in contact over you."

I gaze into the phone, wondering what the man on the other end, looks like, what he's like, who he really is. "Tell my father I want to meet him," I tell Harry Gorney. "From the way I look at it, it's a win-win proposition. The best-case scenario is that I've found a new friend. The worst is that at least I know who I came from."

Another torturous week follows. Every phone call sends me up the wall and through the ceiling. When the call finally comes, it is not a ring ripe with impending consequence as when Harry Gorney had called. Yet on some level, deep down inside, I know that this is no phone call from a stranger.

"Is Jeffrey there?" a soft-spoken male voice asked.

"This is Jeffrey."

A pause ensues. A very long pause. A pause that is longer than all the pauses since the world began, longer than the longest book.

The odd thing of it is that after weeks of waiting, I have no idea of who the man on the other side of the phone could possibly be. Had I been threatened with pain of torture, I could not have guessed who it was.

"Is this Harry... Harry Gorney?"

"No. This is your father."

I always thought if anyone ever said that to me, I'd dissolve on the spot, disappear into the floor below. All I can think is: *This must be the worst call this man has ever made.*

"I'm very glad to hear from you," I said. "I'm glad you called."

One week later my father came to the brownstone in Brooklyn where I lived. Looking in opposite directions, we shake hands. Slowly, inevitably, we assess each other.

I stare into my own face, plus a few decades that hadn't done any harm and a full head of silver hair. He is of medium height and trim but solid. The first words he utters to me, after all this time, are: "I'd hoped you'd be taller."

I shrug, slightly amused. It is no secret that I am slightly built and perhaps too slender, a virtue onstage that allows me to play imps and younger men with ease. Height notwithstanding, I am very happy to look like my father. We talk. I show him through the house I live in, which is currently under restoration, and I introduce him to my pooch, an irresistible pink-nosed Brittany spaniel who looks like his pedigree is courtesy of Walt Disney.

I like the way my father conducts himself. He is knowledgeable about dogs and houses, and he speaks with authority on both. His lively sense of humor surfaces with ease. He is a charming man, and I can see why my mother had fallen in love with him. I like him! Most of all I give him credit for meeting me. It takes courage. I could have been filled with anger, downright vitriolic, put him on the spot, or summoned demons from a past he'd rather have forgotten.

He made minor apologies about everything, but I tell him that I am glad he is here and to let the past rest. It is behavior governed by neither tact nor grace. I want to know him and for him to get to know me. I want us to be us, to be a unit, to be father and son. Asking for my aunts and uncles, he speaks animatedly and with affection.

"Is Allie still a *pinko*?"

"Uncle Allie is kind of olive-skinned."

My father looks puzzled. I am thinking that of my mother's two brothers, Jack was definitely fair, Allie the darker. Some time later I would find out that "pinko" was 1930s slang for being a Communist.

Yes, my mother's brother Allie, very close to her in age, had been one of legions of idealistic Depression-era youth who looked to Russia and its Communist system as an antidote to the nation's financial woes. All of which did not rest well with Grandpa who came from a region that went back and forth from Romanian to Russian sovereignty, a political situation that gave birth to endless ethnic strife.

In Grandpa's world, you either sided with Romania or Russia. He was passionately Romanian with no room for discussion or dispute. For Grandpa, Russia meant the imposition of an unwanted language and a foreign alphabet and culture. For scrappy Allie, it meant imagined economic equality and a better life. Ironically, Allie was a nickname for none other than… Alexander.

Considering Allie's pink disposition and olive skin, an uncomfortable silence follows. Finally my father speaks again.

"Sylvia ever get to first base with the jazz musician?" he asks.

It is apparent that my father memories are of no one I know. He remembers younger versions of people who are my close family and had once been his. I never knew that Allie was a political firebrand or that Cousin Sylvia was ready to give it all up for a vagabond jazz musician. My father is talking about remarkable strangers, other men and women from another time and another place. Finally, he asks for my mother.

"She was a fine woman, your mother. She was a good woman, only too close to her family."

"You mean Betty?"

He shakes his head "yes," and I understand. An unspoken bond forms between us in the unseen presence of my aunt. Much to his credit my father now talks about "rebuilding this family." Yet another family, his new family, and that meant me.

Much to my mother's credit, she had never spoken ill of my father and she forbade anyone else to say a bad word about him. She had allowed me to meet him on my own terms, and I was thrilled. Who meets a father at 30?

I like the way he talks about "this family." I want to become part of it and meet a half-brother and half-sister I had never known.

I would find that they never knew that their father, our father, had been married before. It said a lot that they had not been told about his previous marriage, no less about me. It said more than I wanted to know. Yet I elected to look the other way, and that choice would backfire.

After a brief period of time I met my "new" family. We liked each other. We were all, I can say, mutually eager to discover and embrace each other. My father's second wife, Lee, was somewhat retiring, uncertainly cordial. Lee Gorney once told me that she "never blamed my mother for anything," which I found an odd thing to say, given the circumstances. Again, I look the other way.

During that first meeting, I was struck by something that I doubt the others felt, a simple notion that most people take for granted.

Although we were short of being strangers, my father's other family and I were united by his very being. We all shared his last name, and it wrapped around us like a ribbon. He united us.

My mother's ongoing support of the situation was resonant of her sweet nature and innate common sense. "Whatever he did," she said, "he was your father. I never knew when or if he would re-enter your life." But she imposed one big limitation summed up in three little words: *Don't see Jenny.*

Even my mother's kind spirit could not erase the lasting sting of Jenny's barbed heart. "She was the only person in my entire life," Mom said, "the only person on this earth who was deliberately cruel to me."

Jenny Gorney was still alive, but by all accounts she was possibly next to the oldest surviving woman in the world. Truth be told, I couldn't wait to see her. Maybe it was the actor in me. Maybe it was the writer. Maybe, just maybe, her once-in-a-lifetime visit when I was five had become part of her story, and the legend that was Grandma Jenny.

Like all legends, hers was shaped by time. It turns out that time was not kind to Grandma Jenny. Even as it robbed her of mobility and perception it had not mellowed her. When her sons hired a live-in aide to help her out, Jenny tried to beat the woman up.

After that episode, my father took her under his wing. She came to live with him, but she was asked to leave after throwing a pot of boiling water at Lee. Now she lived in a nursing home where she ruled, I was sure, by a reign of ancient terror...or well-worn witchcraft. My father was eager for me to meet her, and I could not resist.

We went—my father, my half-brother and I—to see old Jenny in the old-age home. There she sat, blank-faced and shrunken, on the edge of a single bed, a withered version of the statuesque woman I remembered.

"You remember Jeffrey?" my father asked.

Jenny looked at my father. She looked at me. She looked at my half-brother. Confusion colored her face. Then she popped the question.

"How many sons do you have?"

She thought and she thought. She looked at me and shrugged. She looked through my half-brother, then back at me, and her eyes brightened with clarity. She clapped her hands once, and then a single tear streamed down her lined cheek.

"Grandma Jenny speaks five languages," my father said proudly. "She speaks Polish, French, Danish, Yiddish, and English."

Denmark had snuck into the family tree in a way never fully explained to me. Traveling from Poland to the West, the Gorneys had lived in Copenhagen long enough to speak the language, and my father had been born there. With great pride, as if showing off a ribbon-winner, he asked Grandma Jenny to "say something in each language."

Wearing an expression of great and tried patience, Jenny Gorney rises unsteadily from her bed. Regaining composure, she totters to the middle of the room where she pauses for a moment. Striking a pose of theatrical authority, Jenny clasps her hands together and holds them firmly to her breast. I fully expect her to sing. Another breathless moment passes. She looks at my father, at me, and then at my half-brother. Jenny takes a deep breath and then she speaks, in a voice at once raspy and silvery.

Dziękuję she said in Polish.

Merci.

Tusand tak.

Danks.

Then a pause that tantalizes, and...

Thank you!

In five different languages, Grandma Jenny had said "thank you" with the flaw-less air of a box-office legend expecting us to thank her. Now she shuffles back to her bed. Assuming a regal perch at bed's edge, she carefully folds her hands, examines her papery fingertips, and gives us the steely eye. Performance over.

"Jenny was what you call shrewd," Grandpa had said, and he was right. Whatever she was or had been, whatever she had done or failed to do, and whomever she had hurt or at the very least offended, she had at the eleventh hour of her life, triumphed. Before the stage lights dimmed and the final curtain fell, Jenny Gorney took a bow, and she made it clear that she was nobody's fool.

• • •

For the next four years, I proceeded to build a relationship with the father I never knew and thought I had lost. I thoroughly enjoyed my half-siblings, and it thrilled me to hear them referred to as "your brother" or "your sister."

With time, however, disenchantments arose. When his other children asked my father why he hadn't done more for me, he answered that my mother kept him from seeing me. He had lied his way out of a tight spot at the expense of my mother, who at the very least—or very best—had protected his reputation. And Lee put in her two cents about the child support we received. "That dollar a day came from my salary." That dollar a day didn't pay rent even in the late 1940s.

These and other minor disappointments reached a new high—or low—when I opened in an off-Broadway version of Oscar Wilde's *Salome* at the Bouwerie Lane Theater. Yes, on the Bowery, in the East Village. The play had a four-week run. I invited both sets of parents. My mother and stepfather came on opening night. My father and his wife never came. During the last week of the show, I called them.

Lee, sounding embarrassed, said "Oh, it's such a terrible neighborhood, and we didn't know where we would park the car."

In a flash, I understood something. Had it been my mother, she would have gotten on a train and gone to the show even though it wasn't her child who was performing. She would have made the effort because it was the right thing to do.

I was crushed. I decided to let the relationship atrophy. My father had never sup-ported me properly as a boy, and now he could not manage to come see me in what amounted to free tickets to an off-Broadway show. My mother's words came back to me. "He was a good guy," she had said. "He'd give you the shirt off his back if you were in trouble but he didn't know what it was you do for people that you love."

I began to let the relationship wither, which he complained about. He told my half-brother that he felt I wasn't giving him proper respect and. I wrote him a letter, a polite yet straightforward letter telling him how I felt and how it was. I never heard from him again.

Would life have been easier with him around? Would I somehow have been better?

Everything that is good in me, anything that is special, came from my grandpar-ents. What they gave me he could never have given me.

Most of all I understood something now. My half-siblings asked my father why he hadn't done more for me, but the question should have come from me. I had opted to discount rather than confront our sad beginnings. I wanted things to work.

I believe everyone deserves a second chance and I wanted us to have ours, but I learned a hard lesson. If my father were going to do the right thing he would have done it all along. I don't think that people ever really change, not really, unless galvanized by extreme trauma or compelling circumstances that trigger enlightenment.

Scarlett O'Hara changed, it has been pointed out, but she had the Civil War march through her living room. And she was hungry.

• • •

9

COMING ATTRACTIONS

I am eleven, and Grandma and Grandpa are at a milestone. They have been married for fifty years. Uncle Louie and Aunt Betty are planning a big party. Everyone is excited, and in the weeks before the great day, our phone just won't stop ringing.

Grandpa snatches up the receiver, and from the length of the conversation and his long-suffering silence I know who's on the other end: my vivacious Aunt Rae. Auburn-haired Rae is married to Uncle Mauritz, Grandma's youngest brother, and her only relative to have come to America. After decades of marriage, Rae and Mauritz still behave like lovebirds.

"What's the secret of it all?" I once asked, already a reporter in the making. "Zis iz eet," she replied proudly in her sassy accent. "He treats me like he met me yesterday! Zat is eet." In one brief phrase, my generous aunt had gifted me with her devoted husband's key to long-lasting romance. As a young man in love, I would heed her words, and more than once. It didn't work.

Uncle Mauritz and Aunt Rae are both Romanian-born, and living proof that opposites attract. My uncle had come to the New World to be with my grandmother, the older sister who just about brought him up, and whom he adored. My aunt came here on the wings of adventure, determined to sparkle in a land where the streets glittered with gold.

Mauritz came from cosmopolitan Iasi, first capital of Romania. He told me all about Iasi, or so I thought. One day I would discover for myself how highly Romanians thought of that city, our city. I would beam with pride at how elegantly her manicured boulevards had weathered the sad tides of history. I would also uncover the secrets that stained her marbled halls, and I would realize how wise my gentle uncle was to have come to America.

Rae, on the other hand, came from a small village buried in the green hills outside the city. She said so little about her town that I grew up thinking it didn't have a name. It was, she implied, a backwater so poor and remote it might as well have been on another planet. She waxed romantic about how she had plotted her escape to America, a desire so urgent it brought her to these shores alone at the tender age of 16, a brave girl, starry-eyed and single-minded.

Over and over, she recalled the moment of moments, her entrance onto the crowded streets of immigrant New York, and how she responded to all those people from God-knows-where, pushing their way along sidewalks littered with God-knows-what. "All my life I dreamed what it would be like, America," she said, "and now I ask myself, 'Why for I did it?'"

Silent Mauritz was an observer who spoke sparingly in serene tones, but when he did speak up, it was worth the wait. Effervescent Rae was emotionally volatile and hopelessly vocal. Neither telephone nor distance could diminish the timbre of her voice or its thunderous decibel level. Even in the kitchen, one room away, I could hear her chatter filtered through the phone lines. Sighing patiently and looking pained, Grandpa hands the phone to Grandma: "It's Rae. I have a headache."

"Oh, Aba," Grandma said, with a slight tone of reprimand. "You know better than that. She is so wonderful, a perfect wife, a loving mother. She and Mauritz live together so well. Such happiness."

Grandpa nods. "I love my sister-in-law more than life itself," he said, "but when she talks, she drills holes in my head."

Aunt Rae, it turns out, had business to discuss. Several days later, she would appear in our kitchen to coach Grandma about what to wear and how to look on her Golden Wedding day. Although they are sisters-in-law, Rae is young enough to be Grandma's daughter, a distinction she wears with pride and broadcasts widely. While Grandma remains refreshingly moored in another time and place, Rae seizes every opportunity she can to become utterly modern and thoroughly American.

She is also notoriously vain, and with good reason: for a woman who came from nowhere, Rachel Neistadt is blessed with an instinct for high fashion. A seamstress by trade, she is what Grandma calls "a snappy dresser" and her talent with a sewing machine is legendary.

Uncle Mauritz worked in a shoe factory; his brothers, in Europe, had after all, been shoe manufacturers. My uncle was the last guy on the assembly line, the one who pounded the heel into the shoe. Mauritz might not have held as prestigious a position as his older siblings in the Old Country, but at least he was, in a way, in the family business. He might have been a factory worker, but with his starched white shirts, bow ties, and rimless glasses, Uncle Mauritz looked more like a bank executive.

While Uncle Mauritz hammered at heels, his wife took in sewing. As the world around them crumbled under the weight of the Great Depression, my aunt and uncle prospered. Not one given to shyness, Aunt Rae paraded her good fortune, apparent in a splashy squirrel coat and diamond wristwatch. "When she had it," I once heard Aunt Betty snap, "she flaunted it."

Even jewels and furs could not grant Uncle Mauritz and Aunt Rae immunity from hard times. After a flying champagne cork robbed my great-uncle of sight in one eye, he could no longer work. All of a sudden the Neistadts, along with the rest of America, were not doing so well. But the Great Depression was no equal for my Aunt Rae.

Financed by sheer nerve, Rachel Neistadt opened a dress shop. In its spotless window, she hung a smart Deco shingle that read: *Madame Rae, Alterations.* Reinvented as the enigmatic, distinctly European Madame Rae, my aunt might have been exiled royalty as far as the neighbors knew. Chic and red-haired, she certainly looked the part. In truth, Aunt Rae was as down-to-earth as she was romantic, a warrior mother and wife who had, in the face of economic disaster, turned skill with needle and thread into bread and butter.

Nearly two decades later, Madame Rae sits at our kitchen table, dispensing fashion wisdom to Grandma in a voice that could be heard in Bucharest.

I sit at the table alongside them, drawing a picture of a house with two trees and a sun. I color the treetops Crayola green.

"Clara, my darling, take my advice," I hear Aunt Rae say. "I know Ethel and Lily are going to put lipstick on you, and earrings. Ethel told me she's taking you to the beauty parlor. They'll make you look like you never looked before. They'll bring out your eyes. You have such lovely eyes."

My grandmother wanders over to the small mirror mounted on the pantry door. She looks at herself. I wonder: does she see in the mirror, even for a moment, young blonde Clara of Iasi? Grandma places one hand to her face.

"I have eyes," she whispers,

"Clara! Don't be silly. You have eyes as blue as the river in Iasi."

I grab a blue crayon and color the sky.

"Take my advice, Clara, I'm young enough to be your daughter," Aunt Rae preened at the thought of her constant, if relative, youth. "Let me tell you something, darling, about the beauty parlor. Tell the girl you're going to a *friend's* Golden Wedding."

Grandma shrugs and walks slowly to the stove.

"You know why? Because if you tell them it's your Golden Wedding, they'll make you look like an old lady."

I wonder what would happen if I color the sun purple.

"I am an old lady," Grandma says, turning on a burner under the aluminum teakettle.

"Clara, darling, I'll make you an outfit, you'll look like when you came here from England. Remember, Clara, I was a sample maker. I made Ethel's wedding dress."

"A lot of good it did her."

"But, Clara, the dress was a beauty. You remember how my Sylvia looked when she won the talent contest. I made that outfit, too."

"The contest. Mauritz didn't like that contest."

I put the purple crayon down, and I listen.

"Mauritz!" Aunt Rae went on. "He said to Sylvia: 'Only you could go to Coney Island and end up singing on the beach with two Italians and a mandolin.'"

"They were nice boys."

"Beautiful boys. How they sang! But the agent, he don't like nobody's names. Vinnie and Sal he changed to the Troubadours. You ever heard of such a word? And Sylvia, from Sylvia Neistadt they made Gypsy Nigh. Hair Sylvia had, black as coal, just like Mauritz when he was young. She looked like a Gypsy alright."

"The *Tziganes*, they knew how to sing," Grandma said. "And the fiddles."

When I was very little I thought Sylvia was Spanish. She was always singing stuff like *Tangerine from the Argentine* and *South of the Border*, and she wore hoops in her ears and had big dark hair. But the hot number, the one she gave her all to, was 100% American: *Sunny Side of the Street*! But somehow, somewhere along the line *Sunny Side of the Street* gave way to *Stormy Weather*.

Uncle Louie said that Sylvia had at last found "her" song.

"It suits her," Mommy agreed.

I can still see Sylvia, in her kitchen and in our living room, and at every wedding and bar mitzvah, standing tall, head back, hands reaching for the moon, voice bouncing off the ceiling…

Don't know why

There's no sun up in the sky.

Aunt Rae and Grandma are still smiling at each other. I guess they are remembering the Gypsies.

"Clara," Aunt Rae continued, "You remember, Clara, you came to see Sylvia sing … at the movie theater downtown."

Grandma looked blank.

"Clara! The theater, with the gold pictures and the big stairs, like where the king lives. You remember. I made Sylvia a white silk top like a sailor suit, with blue sequins on the edge and stars on the flaps. What she looked like. And how she sang."

Grandma shrugged.

"Clara. It was the War. She sang *The Apple Tree*, and—uh—*Praise the Ammunition*. Boom boom boom boom."

"So," Grandma said, "nothing happened."

"Clara, my darling, everything happened. There was that agent, gave them a contract. But Mauritz said to the agent: 'You want my daughter to go on the road? Either the whole family goes, or nobody goes.'"

The teakettle whistles. I consider my drawing pad and that empty circle of a sun waiting to be filled.

"It's better this way," Grandma said, pouring water into glasses where teabags lay, expecting to be drowned.

I take a yellow crayon in hand. The empty sun is waiting.

"It's better," Grandma said. "Sylvia got married."

Aunt Rae sits down with a thud. "Eh," she said, as if swallowing something sour. The yellow crayon freezes in my hand. I glance up. I have never before seen my great-aunt look sad.

"It's better!" Grandma said again.

Aunt Rae's eyes look into mine. We've got a secret. I know why my lively aunt is so suddenly sad. Deep in her heart, Aunt Rae weeps for her daughter and the singer she might have been. Sylvia, who answers every question you might ask with a band song from her past. Sylvia, who sings her soul out at every family function, and the dinner table. Sylvia, who married Al, her mirror image, a man who shares her passion for dancing and chasing dreams. What a tango they did. Sylvia who always made an entrance, looking like a million bucks although she never had a dime.

I know in the very deepest part of me that in the deepest part of her, my aunt cries for the crushed dreams that dim her daughter's shining presence.

I put the crayon down, and I consider the sun.

• • •

10
RARE GOLD

G randma and Grandpa's party is going to be a real shindig. I had heard them talking. They call it a Golden Wedding. Uncle Louie and Aunt Betty have rented a hall and orchestra. Even Aunt Lily, whom I'd never met, would be there, all the way from California.

Lily had moved to Long Beach as a bride in the 1930s. She and my Uncle Irv were supposed to be out West for only a year, Mom told me, but they stayed there for the rest of their lives. Train trips cross-country then and in the decades that followed were pricey, so visits were rare. Phone calls, no different. Once a year, at Passover, when the family gathered together, Lily would call. Because of the expense, talk time was at a premium.

"Hi Lil," Mother would whisper into the phone, her voice choked with emotion. Before she could get a word in, Uncle Louie would shout to Betty, who was usually in the kitchen: "Lily's on the horn!" This was a rallying cry; the shout heard round the holiday dinner table, the opening of the telephone Olympics that pitted me against my three younger boy cousins.

Since I was the oldest, I got to speak first. "Hello, Aunt Lily," I would shout into the phone, trying to make the most of our precious moment while warding off the next in line: small, spirited Cousin Stevie, who would kick and punch me under the table to distract me.

"Jeff!" Aunt Lil would scream into the long-distance line, as if I were in China. She always seemed surprised and delighted to be talking to me. I knew she didn't sound that way with the others.

Every year, it was the same. Before I could answer her, Stevie would snatch the phone out of my hand. "Hello, Aunt Lillian," he would proclaim with the phony air of a well-behaved rich boy. "How are you?"

Uncle Irv never got on the phone. For years, I was convinced he was mute or suffered from an extreme speech impediment, the sad relative we were all ashamed of.

At fifteen, I got to know him better than anyone else ever did. Mom and I planned to move to California, and for one year she stayed in New York to settle business matters while I lived with my aunt, uncle, and Cousin Howard in Long Beach. I lived in a one-family house that was unattached to other houses. My neighbors had names like Smith, Jones, and even Anderson. I might as well have been on a TV series. It was in California that I discovered the truth about Irv's silence. Uncle Irv, unlike the rest of us, spoke only when he had something worthwhile to say.

As a boy, I knew Lily and Irv the way I knew my father—through mail, stories, and photos. Lily writes her letters on paper that is as thin as the skin of a peeled onion. Across the flimsy envelope in a blaze of red are stenciled two little words that set me on fire. AIR MAIL! Stamps of silver planes, wings spread wide and propellers twirling, are alive with the promise of adventure. Can you imagine such a thing? A letter so important and from so far away it has to be carried to Brooklyn by plane. For all I know California is made up. My faraway relatives might be living in Persia, Tibet, or Ancient Egypt.

Aunt Lily lives for me too in my growing collection of picture postcards. Her cards show me what life in California is really like. My favorite is a photo of a gleaming white mansion, probably like the house my aunt and uncle live in. A circle in the upper right-hand corner holds a picture of a pretty brown-haired movie star. The border of the postcard reads: *Home of Dorothy Lamour, star of Paramount Pictures.*

With her shiny brown hair and big brown eyes Dorothy Lamour reminds me of someone, but I can't put my finger on it. I file her away in the shoebox that houses my other postcards, next to the one with the mansion that belongs to Mickey Rooney, star of MGM pictures. More cards follow with scenes that tempt the senses. Multi-colored photos show groves of plump and perfect oranges, long sunny boulevards lined with swaying palms, and a big garden with rows and rows of berry bushes.

Sometimes, if you look hard enough, you can find unexpected treasure buried in letters. Or in snapshots, like the ones that Mom holds up for all of us to see of pictures from Long Beach. No one says anything. We just look and try to imagine how our relatives live outside of Brooklyn; in a far place, in glamorous, golden California. One photo shows a spacious backyard of flowering fruit trees. In the rear you can see the wall of a white house, exactly like the one that Dorothy Lamour owns.

In front of the house stands Cousin Barbara. Small and dainty with ribbons in her hair and holding a pail, Barbara seems to look right at us. Uncle Irv is crouching on the ground, behind her, smiling. He is leaning over a row of plants. In his gloved hand he holds a spade. He is balding with high cheekbones, a dark mustache, and a stern look that, I would come to find out, masked a wondrously kind heart. Mom flips the photo over. On the back, Lily has written: *Barbara plants spittoonias with her Daddy.*

Mother slides the picture aside to reveal the next photo. Baby Howard, wrapped in a blanket held by my aunt, who smiles down at him with dark brown hair piled high on her head, Dorothy Lamour-style. Mom calls it an upsweep. A whole bunch of snapshots follow showing Lily and Irv dancing in clubs, which was something they liked to do. Mom told me that when Uncle Irv was younger, he was a boxer. Then he became a guy who tailored uniforms for sailors so that they fit just right. My mom also told me that when Uncle Irv wasn't boxing or tailoring, he was dancing. I am sure the picture shows my aunt and uncle in a ballroom. I had heard Mom say that Irv, like Uncle Louie, was a ballroom dancer. Now his wife fairly danced her way into our foyer.

"Jeff! My Jeff!" Aunt Lily bubbled, just the way she did on the phone. Her brown eyes sparkle. Spangled bracelets dangle from her wrists as she moves. I knew it. My aunt has long brown hair, glamorous shiny jewelry, and an easy smile.

Now I know what I have always known, from the moment that first postcard came, courtesy of Paramount Pictures. Now I know the real reason my aunt couldn't come east as often as we would have liked. My aunt is Dorothy Lamour. I never tell anyone, not even my closest friends.

I run to Aunt Lily and know at last what it is like to be kissed and hugged by a movie star from California, no less a middle sister. That's what Mom called her, since she was six years older than Mom and nine years younger than Betty. In time to come I would learn what that age difference meant. Lily knew a lot.

During my year in California, Aunt Lily would become an ally and someone I could really confide in. Because she could remember stuff from way back when, Lily is an invaluable and uncensored source of family information.

"Say 'hello' to Cousin Howard!" Aunt Lily said, pulling my little cousin behind her. I am eleven. He is seven. He looks like a monkey. I don't even know him. He is just a kid, a little nobody, and now he's my sidekick.

• • •

11

ALL BRIDES ARE BEAUTIFUL

When I think of that day now, I think of it as a dress rehearsal. In the kitchen, Mom holds a mirror for Grandma to see herself all done up, hair piled high, lips and cheeks waiting to be painted. Aunt Rae claps her hands in joy. Grandma clucks in dismay. Aunt Lily approaches, twisting open a shiny tube of lipstick, and Grandma winces.

"We'll have to hold Mama down," Lily says while applying the pink stick to my grandmother's pursed lips. "Now these," Mom says, taking a pair of earrings she calls "pearl drops" out of a velvet case. I hold my breath and watch as snowy pearls begin to fall from Grandma's ears. "And these," says Aunt Rae, opening a box of long gloves. "Black lace," observes Lily. "Opera gloves," says Mom. "Hoo-ha," says Grandma, gingerly sliding her lean arms into the gloves, as Aunt Rae eagerly helps.

"Stand up," says Mom, "let's take a look." Grandma rises and strikes a pose. Rae fidgets with the hem of the dress, and Lily puts a finishing touch on makeup. Mom fastens the clasp on a string of pearls she has placed around Grandma's neck. "Maybe too much," Lily says, stepping back.

I watch the three women fussing over Grandma. Usually it is the other way around. I look at Grandma, as she contemplates the intricate pattern of black lace on her long and elegant gloves. She looks up at me and smiles a shy smile. I know that smile as no one else does. I know what she is thinking. We've got a secret. I know what no one else in the room knows. Not Aunt Lily. Not Aunt Rae. Not even Mom.

What was it like, Grandma? When you got married. When you and Grandpa were a bride and a groom?

Rain fell lightly in the alley outside our kitchen the day I asked that question on an afternoon that seems lost in time. No one else was in the house, no one but Grandma and me. There was a silence in the air. Misty grey shadows spilled in through our kitchen window.

Weddings were on my mind because Aunt Henny's older daughter was about to get married, and everyone had been talking about it. Weddings, which the grownups called "affairs," were a mystery to me. I was too young to ever be invited. Teenage neighbors babysat me while my grandparents and my mother went off to what they called "halls," fabulous places with glamorous names like Twin Cantors, Fontainebleau, and Kameo Gardens. They always got so dressed up. I could only imagine what went on at a wedding.

What was it like, Grandma? The day you got married?

I watched her beat egg and flour and butter in a wooden bowl. Cinnamon and sugar fell through her fingers like a rain of sweet spice, followed by a shower of salt. Aunt Henny said that Grandma baked by magic. Measuring spoons did not exist for her. Nor did thermometers. Years later, trying to get recipes from her would become a source of endless frustration.

How much sugar do you put in, Mrs. Cohen? How much cinnamon?

Just enough, Henny.

How long do you bake it, Mama?

You bake it, Ethel, till it's done.

Orange honey dripped lazily off a big wooden spoon into the mix. She was making a honey cake for Rosh Hashanah, the Jewish New Year.

"What?" she said absently as she beat the mix into a silky paste.

"When you were married? What was it like?"

"When I was married," she sighed, pouring batter into a pan, which she slid into the oven. I watched her place her hand inside the oven to feel if the heat was right. She might as well have been cooking garlic sausages in a tile stove in Romania.

"Yes, when you were married. Your wedding. When you were a bride."

Grandma wiped her eyes with her apron, as if clearing the way to the past, and she sat down at the table. Our kitchen turned toasty and sweet smelling, while honeyed dough rose slowly in the oven.

"When I was married," she sighed. "When I was married I wore a white satin dress with long white gloves." Grandma held out her hands. Bone thin they were, the limbs of a refugee from life. She looked at her knuckles swollen with arthritis.

"I was beautiful," she said, turning her hands to examine them. "All the brides they are beautiful. It's something inside."

She was a small woman my grandmother was. More than petite, beyond slender, but arms and legs ravaged by illness that struck swiftly and with unexpected power.

It was 1934, or '35, or maybe '37. It was autumn and she was alone in that apartment on Bushwick Avenue where my mother grew up. Perhaps honey cake baked in the oven then. Perhaps its pleasing scent filled that kitchen years ago, just as it did now, with the promise of a sweet new year. In the bedroom, my grandmother knelt while making the bed. Suddenly she stiffened. She could not rise. She could no longer move. She had, she would later say, turned to stone. Now came my mother, home from high school, or was it work, to find her mother/my grandmother frozen in place.

Scleroderma was the culprit, a condition that will make skin tighten with merciless reliability until it strangles a vital organ. Treatments were early and not effective. After a long stay in the hospital, Grandma was told that she might live for maybe five years, perhaps ten, but only if she took it easy…and if she was lucky.

"Taking it easy" was not part of my grandmother's vocabulary nor was maid service or kitchen help. Home from the hospital she cooked and cleaned and shopped. She scrubbed and she laundered and she made it her business to appear at 5:30 in the morning at the baker's door to make sure her family had the freshest rolls and bread.

A decade later, Grandma began to raise me, a boy of eighteen months, even as she tended to the needs of her aging husband, her divorced daughter, the apartment we lived in, and the well-being of her neighbors. She prayed for everybody in the family, every Friday night, prayers tailored to every son and daughter and in-law and grandchild, in fractured English over candles from her lips to God's ears.

Scleroderma or not, my grandmother would live to 88. Her first born, my Uncle Jack, was 17 years older than Mom. He remembered a lot from when he was a boy. He remembered nickelodeons, the first movie theaters, where you paid a nickel to see a silent film. He remembered horse-drawn streetcars rattling along cobblestone streets. He remembered when there were no telephones, and he carried messages back and forth from Uncle Mauritz to a girl he liked. A little on the plump side but pleasing, Mauritz thought, a Romanian named Rachel. She was the girl he would marry. She was my Aunt Rae.

Uncle Jack also remembered Grandma when she was young. She was shapely, he said, pantomiming a womanly curve with his hand. In my day, she was a fragile old lady who wore dark tan stockings around her bandy legs to hide skin spotted tan by an uncommon disease.

None of it put a damper on her lively nature or her affection for dancing. At the least expected moment, she would lower the flame on the stove, put a lid on the pot, curtsy demurely, and break into a little step.

"Did I ever tell you about the dances in Stefanesti, in the town square? We had a band and music. A dress I wore, I will never forget. The color of the sky it was. Boys used to ask me to dance," she said, in a suddenly secretive voice.

"Oh, how I loved to dance," she sighed. Casting a knowing glance toward the heavens, as if speaking to a long-gone beau, she would put her hands on her hips and laugh aloud: "It's the Romanian in me," she would say.

I looked at her ancient stringy arms on the table before me on that vanished rainy afternoon. I tried to picture those arms when young and soft, enveloped in lengthy white satin gloves, the gloves of a bride.

"My wedding dress was beautiful," Grandma went on. "Did I tell you I carried a fan at my wedding, a big fan with white feathers."

She leaned forward, confiding in me what I knew she had not told any other grandchild, perhaps not another being in all the years.

"We were married in the garden in front of the house in Iasi. We went off in a carriage, with white horses."

"White horses!" I gasped. "Where is the wedding dress, Grandma? Can I see it?"

"No."

"Why not? Do you still have it?"

"I don't have it."

"Well, where is it?"

"I cut it up to make dolls for my daughters," she said, as casually as if she had shredded a book of unused coupons.

I wondered even then what she felt in her heart, in our kitchen in Brooklyn, when she spoke of that silky dress, stitched and sewn and worn proudly in Iasi so many years ago. I wondered if the bride she had been, radiant with love and hope, still danced somewhere inside her soul.

I thought of my grandparents in England where they had lived and prospered before moving to America. Where, Grandma had said, her taste was so respected that neighbors and friends and especially new immigrants sought her advice on what to wear on which occasion and how to furnish their homes.

My grandma, the grandmother I knew, turned her back on fashion and saw furniture and knick-knacks as objects to be endured, created solely for the dust cloth. How did she go from success and style to denial and modesty? How did she get here from there? Why did she and my grandfather leave England? Did it have to do with the little girl they lost, the aunt whom I would never meet?

I wondered about Goldie. No one ever spoke of her. I doubt any of my cousins knew she had ever existed. She had died too young, and under circumstances never recalled. Once I heard Aunt Betty talking to Mom about it. She said there had been an inquest. I did not know what that meant but it sounded awful.

• • •

Even so Goldie's presence haunted our house. She looked at us out of the past in a photo from the old days, a pretty little girl, blond and dear in her little dark shiny dress. Was it a deep red brown, like roasted tea leaves, or was it the color of red wine, or what they call maroon? Or maybe it was just plain black as a licorice stick? It was hard to tell because the photo was so ancient and shaded by a pale brown tint, the way those photos used to be. But you could see how bright the stripes were that ran along the hem of the skirt and the sleeves, as sunny as Goldie's hair.

So crisp was the material that the dress looked like it was going to dance. Grandma said it was made of something called taffeta. Was it the same dress Goldie wore on the day she died? A special dress worn on her last day on earth, to celebrate the day life left her, and in such an awful way, a day and a death that changed every-thing for all of us.

It is funny, but when I look at that picture, I think of something else. Grandma always talks about the color of Goldie's hair, and when I was little and my hair was yellow, she called me Golden Boy.

Yes, it is all kind of funny. I wonder what my grandmother had been like, as a bride in Romania and as a fashionable young wife and mother in England, long before she grew old and wore time on her face instead of powder, and had no use for style at least for herself. Her wedding dress was a clue.

Many years later, when Cousin Sylvia died, right after the funeral, we were going through her photo album. There was Sylvia, captured on film: a dark-haired girl of 12 or 13, standing in front of the stoop in Brooklyn. Then, in a volunteer nurse's uniform during World War II, quietly determined yet proud; Sylvia, from the same era, a flower in her hair, posing with a sailor, hand on his hip, looking cocky the way they did.

There was Sylvia the bride, aloof and majestic, gliding down the aisle, flanked by Uncle Mauritz and Aunt Rae, both looking concerned. I follow the wide angle of the photo as it sweeps across the hall. One by one, rows and rows of guests enter my field of vision. They all face the bride. Scanning the group, seeking someone familiar, I find myself looking at strangers, or at younger versions of aged relatives and family friends.

In the lower right-hand corner, I notice an especially fine-looking woman. Her hair is brushed back in a gracious twist. Large oval earrings bespeak choice and good taste. No doubt a woman of importance, her handsome face made all the more impressive by visible intellect and certain accomplishment.

"Who is that?" I ask aloud.

"Don't you know?" said Mother, looking over my shoulder.

Tears begin to well in my eyes. It is Grandma, looking for all the world like the woman she might have been if life had been kinder to her.

In years to come, as I began to uncover the buried stories of my family's past, I would find that the woman my grandmother might have been, in fact, she once was.

• • •

12

HIDDEN SECRETS

"There's buried treasure in this house," I said to Howard, looking over my shoulder to make sure the coast is clear. In the kitchen, Grandma continues to look martyred as Aunt Rae tugs at her hem, and Mom and Lily bustle around. "Come with me," I said to Howard. "I'll show you."

Crafty as a fox, daring as a boy detective, I usher my little cousin out of the foyer, into the living room, and up to the credenza. I nod toward the top drawer. "This is a forbidden place," I announce. Howard's face breaks into an elastic smile. I direct his gaze toward the drawer's pulls. His hazel eyes wide open, cast a look of wonder my way as well as concern. Two lions' heads, ominous in pewter, stand guard at either side of the polished mahogany drawer. "Open this, if you dare," they seem to say.

The credenza is what Mom calls a catchall. You never know what you'll find in there. I finger the metal rings that hang heavily from the lions' mouths. I tug at the pulls. "Wow!" Howard gasps. "You have to be very careful," I explain, slowly sliding the drawer open. Worried excitement flickers across Howard's face.

"Behold," I said, opening the drawer even further. A dramatic sweep of my hand reveals an unexpected stash of rare and mystifying riches: an ancient telegram, a stained menu, a corsage of pink string and sugar cubes turned grey and brittle with age (leftover, my mom had said, from her sweet-sixteen party). Here, a faded post-card marked with a blue Star of David asks for donations to build an orphanage in the new State of Israel. There, a tarnished key chain from Atlantic City in its heyday.

"Saloon girls!" Howard cried. "No," I explained, picking up the big menu. A colorful painting on the front showed a beautiful lady, lifting a ruffled skirt to show off her long naked legs and silver slippers. I point to the fancy blue lettering on the side of the card: "See what it says? "

Howard shrugged.

"Latin Quarter!" I read with authority.

"What's that?"

"It's a nightclub. It's where Uncle Louie takes Aunt Betty at night." I open the menu. Scribbled inside, in bold handwriting, are the words: "To Jeff. How dy'a do." Signed: *Jimmy Durante*, a popular comedian on TV. Uncle Louie seemed to know all the stars personally, and he was so close to Durante that he called him by his first name. "Jimmy was in great form that night, Jeff," he told me. "A frustrated vaudevillian," that's what Mom called Uncle Louie.

My frustrated uncle loved to entertain at family gatherings, along with Cousin Sylvia, and he could really put over a song. Uncle Jack accused Sylvia of being a belter. It was true her voice could make the walls of a room move back, but she sang the words like she really meant them, and when she took that mike in her hand and stood in front us, it was something to see. Uncle Jack said that even when Sylvia entered a room "the cameras were always rolling."

Louie had a different style. He would warble gently in soothing tones. Mom called him a crooner, kind of like Bing Crosby, she explained. She said Louie was a period piece, whatever that meant. With his slicked back black hair, she said, and his smart suits, and silky voice, you could picture Uncle Lou standing in front of one of those bulky, old-fashioned radio mikes.

"For all the money Louie made in girls' sportswear," Uncle Jack had once said, "the only time I ever saw him look really happy was singing in front of a crowd making love with his voice to the microphone in his hands." Years later, I would remember that, and Uncle Jack was right.

When Uncle Louie took Aunt Betty to those glamorous nightclubs, he always asked the performers for autographs using me as an excuse. Then he'd give the signed menus or postcards to me. Uncle Louie's pal Jimmy Durante lived for me on the Latin Quarter menu in the forbidden credenza drawer right next to a card from the Copacabana, another New York hot spot. Howard liked that one the best. It had a picture of another beautiful lady.

No legs, oh no. All you could see was her face, big and bold, with juicy red Valentine lips and a pile of fruit on her head that seemed a mile high. On the backside of the card, in ballpoint ink, someone had written: "Best Wishes. Sonja Henie." She was also Uncle Louie's friend. He called her Sonja, and he said that she had been a champion skater who later danced on ice in the movies. These days, she did it in nightclubs. Sonja, he said, had been born and brought up in Norway. It always impressed me how he not only knew all these famous people by their first names, but where they came from and what they did. I moved Sonja to the left.

"Look at that!" Howard gasped. "It's a hundred years old." Peeking out from right under Sonja Henie was a yellowing piece of paper that I had never seen before. Fancy script, once wet with ebony ink, still shone clearly. I skimmed the writing and my eye shot down to the bottom of the document. I read those words, written so long ago, and gasped.

Certificate Received from Wynne E. Baxter, Coroner for County of London; Witness my hand, this 7th day of December, 1909.

"What is it?" Howard asked.

"I don't know. Just an old piece of paper."

I didn't know. All I knew for sure was that the forbidden credenza drawer had unexpectedly surrendered one of its deepest, darkest secrets: the death certificate for Goldie, the aunt I would never know.

"Do you ever think about her?" I had asked Grandma, one day after school, on an afternoon when for some reason my grandmother had been talking about London. Maybe it was the endless rain.

"Of course I think about her. Even after all these years not a day goes by that I don't think about her."

"Did you cry? Did you cry when it happened?"

"I cried. I cried till there were no tears. They watched me, they were afraid I would do something to myself. Your Grandpa's heart, it broke his heart. She was the light of his life."

"What did you do after you cried. Did your heart break, too?"

Grandma's voice lowered, as if she were sharing a very special secret. "I cried and I cried," she said, "but I realized that I had other children, and that they needed me."

My eye moved down to the next line of dark and flowing script, written a lifetime ago by a forgotten man on another continent. A single word jumped out, gripped my throat, and seized my heart.

Inquest

Such a murky word it was, shrouded in the unknown, and steeped in fear.

Inquest

"What's going on?" Howard asked, worried.

Inquest, I read to myself. ... *Held, December 9th, 1909.*

I had a notion of what the word meant.

Aunt Betty said there had been an inquest held after Goldie died. Goldie had been a few years younger than Betty, in England. No one ever talked about her, or how she died, and an inquest could not have been a thing to be desired.

Mom said that Goldie's sudden death and the terrible inquest that followed had destroyed Grandma and Grandpa. "They fell apart," she said. I read on, balancing and weighing the words on the yellowed document.

Death... caused by burns inflicted while dusting the mantelpiece looking glass.

So that's how little Goldie died. One part of the mystery solved, it would seem. But even then I had my doubts. Why would a three-year-old girl be dusting the mantel, especially when the fire was lit? Was she playing house? Was she being punished for being bad and made to do housework, like Cinderella? Or had she been ordered to dust the fireplace by Grandpa's mother, who lived with them, and who had a reputation for being strict? Why was little Goldie alone? Where were the grownups when tragedy struck?

"You're hiding something!" Howard squealed.

"No, I'm not," I said, aware of the responsibility I now assumed. I was the keeper of privileged information. Feeling supremely adult, I said simply to Howard: "You're too young to understand."

All the time I wondered to myself: "What was an inquest?" I kept thinking and thinking about Goldie. Grandma said she liked to dress up and especially to wear Grandma's shoes. I pictured her, small and sweet. She had, I was told, blond hair and blue eyes. She was the prettiest, Grandma had said, of all the children. I wondered if they thought that because she had died so young. I wondered what she was like, and what would have happened to her, to us, if she had lived.

Years later, when we talked about it, my mother said she had always thought Goldie would have been diplomatic like Uncle Jack, gentle and kind like Grandma, super-smart like Grandpa, and the perfect older sister who would have created a buffer between Mom and spitfire Betty.

I was sure that Goldie would have gone a different path than the others. She loved to dance, they said, and I had no doubt, had she lived, my grandparents would have stayed in England. By the late 1920s Goldie Cohen would have been a young woman. She would have changed her name, I was certain, from Goldie Cohen to something more glamorous, like ... Gilda Kane! My Aunt Goldie, had she lived, given her lively nature and passion for dancing, would have been a silent screen star or an adored music hall legend: Gilda Kane, the toast of Mayfair.

I close the credenza drawer, locking the sad death certificate away, spinning daydreams all the while about what little Goldie would have been and might have done had she lived. Who would ever know?

There is a knock at the door.

• • •

13
A BELOVED VISITOR

"**Y**ou know this lady?" Grandma asked, pointing to heavyset Helen who had just settled onto the sofa, pale grey cushions puffing up around her and threatening to swallow her. She sighs in great comfort. You wouldn't know she was sinking.

Did I know this lady? Grandma was being devilish and it made me angry. Well, maybe she meant it for the benefit of Howard, who stood behind me. "Of course, I do," I said. This is Cousin Helen, for God's sake. Mom calls her one of our favorites. I run to her, and Helen leans a head full of fine curly grey hair toward me for her customary kiss.

It is hard to believe but Grandma told me that when they first met, right after Grandma had come to America, Helen was what Grandma called a "skinny Minnie."

I had seen pictures of Helen when she was young, and I know it is true. There she is, peering at the lens, a slender reed of a girl in what looks like angel's robes. No more than 14 or 15 at the time, she is one of the few people who were around when everything about the Old Country was still new. Like Aunt Lily, she is an eyewitness to the past, a source of long-forgotten and highly valued information. I turn around to my kid cousin from California, and with the pride of close acquaintanceship, I say: "Howard, this is your cousin Helen."

Helen beams at Howard, and insists upon initiating him into the let's-kiss-Helen club. "Oh, *tante*," Helen said, "they look like brothers." Then she and Grandma begin jabbering in Yiddish, obviously about Howard and me. Finally Helen takes out a hanky and wipes her brow. "Where is Lily? I'm dying to see her, and Ethel?"

"Shopping. With Rachel," Grandma answered. "They didn't like the gloves."

"And Uncle?"

"He went around the corner to get the paper."

"With all the preparations for the *simcha*, he goes to get the paper!"

"It's his pleasure. Wait, we'll have some tea."

While Grandma heads for the kitchen, Helen begins to shower attention upon me and Howard.

"So, how are you enjoying your visit, Howard?"

"It's okay. We found a certificate in the drawer for somebody who died in England."

Helen looks startled. I'm not sure if it's because of the thought of the death certificate or the sudden clatter of glasses and plates in the kitchen.

"Goldie, huh?" I asked.

"It was a terrible tragedy." She shrugged. "Even so, you should have seen your grandparents when they came here."

"Tell me about them, Helen," I had once asked her on a crisp autumn day, a day when Grandma had gone out for a carton of milk, leaving us alone together. It had flashed through my mind that a long time ago, Grandma had done the same thing in England. A blameless, actually a selfless, act. Gone out to the corner for a bottle of milk, and returned to the sweet little house on Redmans Road, to find her life changed forever.

What were Grandma and Grandpa like when they first came here? When they were young?

"Well, Uncle Aba came over first. That was the custom. The man would come to find work and a place to live, and when everything was set he sends for the wife, and the rest of the family...sometimes, one by one. The children who were left behind in Europe, the 'paper children.'"

I looked at her, puzzled.

"Remember, Jeffrey, there were no phones, no telegrams. So because they kept in touch with their kids by writing, they called them 'paper children.'"

"Well, what happened was, your grandfather arrived a day or two earlier than expected." Howard and I pull up our chairs to listen. With her plump, heart-shaped face, and calm voice, Helen could tell a story almost as well as Grandpa. Like Grandpa, she could tell the same story over and over without ever changing a word, and it always seemed like she was telling it for the first time. But I had never heard this one before.

Helen wiped her brow again. Out of the corner of my eye, I see Grandma standing in the living room doorway, smiling. Helen doesn't seem to notice her.

"Well," she went on, "I was sitting on the stoop with my friend, Libby Wiederhorn. Suddenly little Libby looked up the street and gasped. "Who's that!"

"Who?" I asked.

"That man. He looks like a matinee idol."

"'That man?' That man is my Uncle Aba. Boys, my heart fluttered. Remember, in those days, in the neighborhood we lived in. immigrants came over from Europe by boatloads. Every Monday and Wednesday, someone new came to the street. They were poor. They dressed funny. They couldn't speak English. They were what we called greenhorns. From mud huts in Russia they came, from caves in Italy. They looked foreign. They sounded foreign. Sometimes they smelled foreign!

"Well, your grandfather, he wore a pinstriped suit and a Panama hat, and he was so tall and so handsome. I had lost my heart to that picture we had of him. But boys, the picture didn't do him justice. And then he spoke."

'Pardon me, do you know where the Cohens live?'

"Well, you could hear England in his voice. The way he spoke, so polite. So he was not only handsome, but cultured. I took to my heels and ran inside to get my mother. Before you know it, the months passed, and we went to the ship to meet your Grandma with Jack and Betty."

Howard didn't know what to make of any of this. But I had plenty of questions. *What was Grandma like then? What did she look like? How did she behave, like in Ellis Island and all?*

"First of all, she didn't come through Ellis Island. She arrived with Jack and Betty on a big steamer, tourist class, and they docked uptown. You should have seen her when she came down the gangway. She was wearing a lynx scarf."

Howard and I looked at each other, perplexed.

"Links?" I asked, picturing juicy little sausages strung together around my grandmother's neck.

Helen smiled. "It was a fur," she said, "like a weasel but attractive. And she wore a big hat with an ostrich plume, which was the fashion in those days, and she brought with her a trunk full of English china."

I picture Grandma with a moon-shaped hat of great size and a huge but graceful white feather sticking out of it, pointing right at the sky. I wondered what happened to all the English china, whatever that meant. I looked at Howard ready to exchange knowing smiles, but my expression changed to disbelief. Howard was yawning.

Another time, Helen told me that when the family first saw Grandma appearing on the deck, she held Jack by one hand and Betty by the other. "Suddenly," Helen said, "Betty pulled away from *Tante* and started running down the gangway. A ship's officer picked her up. Assuming she couldn't speak English, he pantomimed that she wasn't allowed to do this.

"Put me down," Betty said in a clipped British accent. "I've come to see my father,"

"I don't know if it was because he wasn't expecting her to speak English, or maybe he just didn't expect such a stern response from such a little girl, but the officer dropped her like a hot potato, and she ran down the gangway, first off the ship."

I clapped my hands and giggled. Helen lit up at my response.

"We laughed, too," she said. "And how your grandfather kissed her. Not just handsome, like I said, but oh so sweet."

"Helen," Grandma called. "Tea is ready."

We all head for the kitchen when the front door flies open with a vengeance.

My "sweet" grandfather stomped into the foyer. He shouted to the room in general and Grandma in particular "Do you know what that son-of-a-bitch told me. He has the Blue-e Creuze." Helen looked mystified. Grandma sighed. I nodded knowingly to Howard, who was totally lost.

"He" was the courtly Mr. Carp, who lived across the street, kitty-corner from us. Other old men in the neighborhood had varied virtues. Mr. Frank wore snappy suspenders. My pal Louis Palermo's grandpa had a turned up nose that looked like he'd slept with a clothespin on it. Mr. Auerbach collared you in the street to sing songs in Russian that no one understood or wanted to listen to. Only Mr. Carp could match Grandpa in wit and style.

Carp's daughter, Mary Roth, pointed out that in many ways the old men were similar. They were both tall, chivalrous, and intelligent. Both spoke several languages. Both were verbal and possessed sly wit.

But to the innocent bystander, the likenesses were lost, especially at Ben and Bess's corner candy store. Mr. Carp read the Morning Journal. Grandpa read the Jewish Daily Forward. They took the opposing positions of the newspapers they each read seriously and fought over it all, on current and historical events, on politics, neighborhood news, and the fate of Jews wherever they might be. Carp was not only a keen adversary, but he had an edge that he never failed to hold over Grandpa.

"He worked ten years longer than I did," Grandpa stormed on. "So he got the health insurance. And the Social Security. Did I know? I thought I was smart. They offered us a choice. Why should I pay extra taxes, I thought. So I didn't get the Social Security. But Carp, he not only gets the checks from Social Security, he has the Blue-e Creuze! Hah! Blue Cross, my eye. What I did in the toilet this morning in ten minutes he didn't do in his whole life."

Grandpa straightened his cooper's cap and whirled about.

"Where are you going?" Helen cried.

"I am going out into the world!"

He opened the door and left with a flourish.

"Where is he going?" Howard asked.

Mr. Carp and Grandpa would each live ten years longer. They would die one day apart, Grandpa passing first. I can still remember redheaded Mary Roth coming to our apartment to break the news about her father.

"Can't you see them up there, arguing," she said to Mom. "Did you think, Ethel, that your father would leave my father behind?"

• • •

14

THE GREAT DEPRESSION

Betty's bombshell entry into America, scampering down the ships gangway in defiance of official rules was no accident. That fiery streak would gain momentum over the years, inspired by monetary gain, at least by our standards, and endless adoration by her husband, my smitten Uncle Louie. All this peaked when she and Louie became the financial safety net for my retired grandparents, and by extension, for us. On occasion, it got out of hand with displays of uppity behavior.

"Whatever Betty and Louis do," Mom said, "Grandma and Grandpa earned."

It was a story not uncommon to the 1930s. At the height of the Great Depression, Uncle Louie lost his job. He and Betty appeared at Grandma and Grandpa's door with their two sons in hand, ten-year-old Norman and six-year-old Hartley.

"There was barely enough room for us," Mom went on. "We lived in a two-bedroom apartment. Grandma and Grandpa had the master bedroom. Aunt Lily and I slept in the smaller bedroom. Uncle Jack and Uncle Allie slept on a foldout sofa in the living room. Betty and Louie and the boys moved in and, you know, no one batted an eyelash. Everything revolved around Norman and Hartley. That's the way it was then, we had less but we did for each other. We looked out for each other."

Now I understand why Norman and Hartley were so close to us when I was growing up. Norman was only seven years younger than Mom, so by the time I was ten or so, he was already married and living in Massachusetts.

My mother and I used to visit him. We would go to Grand Central Station to take the night train to Boston. Making our way through the cars to our seats, we entered into a scene charged with drama. All those passengers sitting upright, some fast asleep, others trying to sleep. You could see suitcases jammed into the small spaces underneath or stuffed into racks above. Some of the people clutched their bags in their arms. Others cradled sleeping children. Still others gazed out the window, searching for signs and borders that had not year appeared. There was only one explanation. Refugees! The truth could not be hidden. Our train rumbled on, racing into the dark.

Norman might have been far away in exotic Boston, but his kid brother Hartley was always around. Hartley was young and dashing, with slicked back dark brown hair. He was in love and newly married, and I wanted to be like him.

I never envied him more than when he would come to our house with his beautiful auburn-haired bride and a sturdy boxer named Dusty. How rugged and handsome that dog was, trotting into our small apartment as if he owned the place. My grandmother called him "Duster."

Hartley bought me a set of electric trains. We worked together creating a home for the set, locomotive to caboose, on a big wooden board in the living room. It was so big that it nearly took over the entire space, turning the small room into a maze of miniature tracks, model villages, and train stations. Signals and signs lit up so that miniature trains could find their way. Whistles tooted into the fake night. It stayed there for a long while.

Four wives and several failed business ventures changed Hartley. Wife number three came and went so fast we never got to meet her, but Mom said we got a great dentist out of her. Time took its toll on Hartley, too. You got the feeling that he was always running from someone. Finally he moved away and we never heard from him again.

My cousin Hartley was a class act. He bought me my bar-mitzvah suit, from Brooks Brothers no less. And he was kind. He gifted me with my first pet, a beautiful blue parakeet.

Grandpa had no use for the bird. When it flew about, it made him nervous. When it would land on his head, he bellowed that his scalp was being ground to dust. One day Pepe took a nosedive into Grandpa's cup of coffee. On the wings of an ungodly shriek, he zoomed out of the cup, white tail feathers turned taffy. Grandpa showed no mercy.

Mom admired Pepe's bright blue beauty, but she understood neither the charm of animals nor the bond between boy and pet. Only Grandma cared.

My grandmother was wonderful with the bird. She became my ally in trying to teach him to speak. We took turns enunciating choice phrases over and over. We taught him his name and address, in the hopes that it would ensure a speedy return should he ever fly the coop, and make it out the window.

"My name is Pepe Gorney. I live at eight twenty five Lenox Road," I would say over and over again, sounding like a prize student in a voice and diction class. Then Grandma would take over. "Mai name Pepee Goornee," she would say over and over in her best and fractured English. "I leef eight twenty fife Lenox Rue."

Against all odds, Pepe acquired a substantial vocabulary that was miraculously devoid of an accent.

I was the guy who fed him but Grandma couldn't wait to help out, and she loved playing with him. Intuitively she allowed the bird to be her guide to the natural world and, I think, to the younger woman, the girl who still lived somewhere inside her.

When Pepe died, she tenderly lifted him up from the cage floor, held him in her hand, put her mouth to his beak, and tried to breathe life into him.

On a brisk autumn day, at the height of Pepe's short but lively life, I was doing homework sprawled out on the living room floor. Grandma was getting ready to leave the house. She put on her coat and she put on her hat. On the way to the front door, she made a short, obligatory detour into the kitchen to say goodbye to the bird. I had entered the room and watched as she pressed her old face against the cage.

Using the Yiddish *faygeleh*, meaning little bird or birdie, she said, with great and instructive affection:

Ta Tah, faygeleh.
That's what we say in England,
Ta Tah!

• • •

15
OLD WEDDING
BELLS

"**S**ay 'Cheese!'" the man behind the camera bellows in a voice as brassy as the yellow polka dots on his big fat black tie. My boy cousins and I grin in silly obedience, all lined up for a Golden Wedding photo. No girls here. Aunt Lily has brought Howard from California, but Barbara stayed behind with Uncle Irv. The only other girl cousin, Eleanor, remains at home in Brooklyn for reasons unknown, foreshadowing future eccentricity. That leaves us, five of Grandma and Grandpa's youngest grand-boys to face the camera together. Spruced up in snappy sport jackets and bow ties, like dapper ducks in a row, we say "cheese," bedazzled by a blinding flash, turning us into Kodak boys forever.

That Golden Wedding is a big success. I get to meet relatives who haven't been around in my short lifetime, but who have been talked about so often that I think I know them.

Cousin Florence works in a Laundromat and takes care of her mother, Tante Becky, whose long-dead husband was Grandpa's youngest brother. They live in a curious place called "the projects" right near the Brooklyn Navy Yard on a street called Navy Walk. Can you imagine such a thing? Florence is what I guess used to be called plain, but Mom said that what Cousin Florence lacks in looks and stuff she makes up for with her good heart.

When Mom was little, she would visit Tante Becky and Florence. They lived in another neighborhood then, and she remembers that Florence would drop whatever she was doing to pay attention to Mom, who was a little younger. Florence would read stories to her, or say, "Let's take a walk around the block." She would make up her own stories about the houses they saw, and the people who lived inside those houses, or about strangers passing by in the street. I wonder why Florence didn't become a writer. I guess she decided to fold towels in the Laundromat instead, and take care of her mother.

While I think about this, I notice Florence smiling at me.

"What do you want to be when you grow up, Jeffrey?" she asks, in the most soothing voice ever.

"A commercial artist."

"Oh you can do it! I'm sure you'll be a success at anything you do."

From the warmth of her voice I know she really believes in me, and I know deep down inside what Mom means when she says that Florence's good heart is more important than her bad luck.

I look around the room, wondering who else is around. There is Cousin Mac who drives a taxi. He is bald with a round face, a skinny mustache, and a big smile. I know Mac because he comes to the house once in a while, and even brings his friends to play cards with Grandpa. Mom says Mac is absolutely adorable "as long as he remembers to keep his false teeth in his mouth." I watch his rubber-band smile with special interest. I hold my breath each time it snaps into action, wondering if his teeth will fall out.

Then there is Cousin Jean. While the others visit us from time to time, Jean never ever comes around. I know all about her, anyhow, and for good reason. Jean is a woman with a past. Whenever they talk about her, my grandparents whisper her name, after which Grandma says, without fail and in hushed tones: "Freie Liebe" (*Free Love*).

I know all about free love. I saw *Ivanhoe* twice. Ivanhoe was a knight who gave his love freely to two damsels, both in distress: Rowena and Rebecca. Jean, it turns out, gave her love freely to one man, who was really in distress: he was married! His wife wouldn't divorce him because she was an Orthodox Jew, and they don't do such things.

Jean and her free-lover Ben run a hotel in the Catskills in a place called Kerhonkson, New York. This hotel is so big that they call it The Grand Palace Kerhonkson. Jean had invited Grandma and Grandpa to visit the hotel, and they stayed there once for an unhappy weekend. It seems The Grand Palace Kerhonkson didn't live up to its name. When Uncle Louie brought my grandparents home, he told us the Grand Palace was so cheap they "sliced the pickles with razor blades."

I wonder which of Ivanhoe's damsels Jean will look like: Rowena or Rebecca. Joan Fontaine played Rowena. They called her "a Saxon woman of great beauty," and she wore a long blonde braid that hung down the front of her long pastel dress. Elizabeth Taylor played Rebecca. She had raven hair and wore a white satin dress and a cap embroidered with a blue Star of David. They called her a "beautiful Jewess," and then tried to burn her at the stake.

I am sure Jean, even though she is a Jewess, will look like Rowena, since there are so many fair-haired people in Grandpa's family. You can imagine my surprise when I finally meet Jean at the Golden Wedding. She wears a braid, all right, but it isn't blonde. It is grey, like the tweed in Grandpa's overcoat, and it doesn't hang down the front of her dress but lassoes the top of her head, like the rope lariats we made at summer camp.

Uncle Allie had a different take on Jean's braid. I am right near him when he whispers that with that braid of hair wrapped round the crown of her head, Cousin Jean looks like a Russian factory worker.

Well, he didn't exactly whisper, in fact he said it just loud enough for Grandpa to hear him.

At the mention of the word "Russian" Grandpa's ears perk up and he just about turns red. Whirling around, he gives Uncle Allie the steely eye.

"Comm-ew-neest!" he bellowed.

Storming toward Allie, he strikes a challenging pose, fists raised and clenched like a boxer about to swing into action. Uncle Jack, usually so quiet, holds Grandpa back, Uncle Allie shrugs,

My attention wanders back to Free Love Jean. I had expected her under any circumstances to be glamorous in the extreme. I hope my disappointment in her plain, if sturdy, appearance doesn't show.

There are two other cousins I have heard a lot about but have never met. I keep scouring the room for them. I tug at Mom's dress.

"Are they here?"

"Who?"

"Gentleman Jim."

"No!"

"Annie Dinkles!"

"Oh, no. For goodness sake, we haven't seen her for years."

Gentleman Jim is the one they call the black sheep of the family. He had paid a surprise visit to us years ago, but I was too young to remember it.

"Ugh, how could you let him into your house!" I had once heard one of the other cousins say to Mom. "He's so dirty!" said another.

I wonder how Gentleman Jim got so dirty and how did he become a black sheep? Gentleman had been orphaned early on and came to live with my grandparents when Mom was little. That's all I know. Oh, and he was a poet, and he was brilliant. He had what they called a photographic memory.

If Gentleman Jim was so dirty and awful, why did they call him "Gentleman?" No information on that one, either. And nothing on Annie Dinkles for that matter. Every time I heard her name, I'd laugh myself silly. I figured with a name like that, she must look like someone out of L'il Abner. Sorta like Mammy Yokum, with funny striped stockings and a mole on her chin with a single whisker sprouting out of it.

I can just see Ol' Annie Dinkles sitting on a porch, or I guess the fire escape, puffing on a corncob pipe. And how did she ever get that name? There are no other Dinkles in the family.

My eyes roam across the room to see how everyone is doing. They look back at me. I smile and wave, even if I don't know who they are, so they will know I am having a good time. People are seated together who have never even met. Aunt Henny and Uncle Nat sit at the same table as Cousin Helen and her husband, Max the dry cleaner. On the other side of the table sit a couple of old ladies from the Old Country. All of them come from Iasi.

Grandma and her old lady friends would always laugh with great pleasure about the old days. They didn't all know each other in Iasi, in Old Romania, but they used to go to the same places over there. They really seem to love the bridges that crossed the river.

They hoot over the Wooden Bridge and chuckle about the Iron Bridge, but it is the Red Bridge that is the big one. They fall quiet when they speak about it. "Die Roite Brig" Grandma calls it in Yiddish, or the *Podu Ros* in Romanian, depending on her mood. From what she tells me, it was quite the place to "meet the boys," as she put it.

I try to imagine Grandma and the others, young and in long dresses, twirling frilly umbrellas as they bat their eyes at dashing young men who lean against the railings of the Red Bridge, young men with suits and vests and watch fobs. Dapper fellows with thick mustaches like Grandpa's.

I picture the Bridge, its metal railings painted a red that catches fire in the sun. Years later, Mom told me she always thought the bridge was made of different size bricks of all shades of red. Bricks that were light, bricks that were dark, crimson bricks, and ruby. Mom's red bricks glittered too in the Romanian sun.

The only thing that puzzles me about the Golden Wedding is that I do not see anything Gold anywhere. The "hall," as they call it, seems gloomy to me. A long dark hall it is, but filled with stuff that is, thankfully, white. Snowy flowers with long petals spill out over tall trumpet-shaped vases made of straw painted white. Cloud-white carnations shimmer in glass bowls on creamy tablecloths.

Grandma and Grandpa are dressed in dark clothes. Grandma, who is usually in what they call a housedress and apron, looks like a duchess. Her hair is done up, and she wears an orchid on her black lace dress. Mom calls that dress a "confection." Grandpa, whom I never saw in anything but plaid shirts, looks really sharp in his charcoal grey suit with a white carnation in the lapel.

My grandparents look so fine that I don't understand why the band plays funny music when they enter the hall. It sounds like hillbilly music to me. The grown-ups all seem to know it by heart, and they all think it is pretty funny, too. They all sing along...

The old grey mare, she ain't what she used to be, ain't what she used to be ... ain't what she used to be ...

"That was probably Louie's idea," I hear Uncle Allie whisper. Whatever, it really got everyone going, all clapping and laughing and tapping their toes. Then these guys roll out a big pink and white wedding cake. Everybody sings "the bride cuts the cake" as Grandma takes a knife in her hand, just the way she does in the kitchen. Only now, instead of slicing onions or peeling carrots, she cuts into that beautiful creamy cake, yellow on the inside and smeared with berry jam.

After a round of applause, Grandpa makes a speech. Some of the ladies dab at their eyes with hankies they take out of shiny black pocketbooks. Grandpa does something then that I never saw him do before. He kisses Grandma! She holds her head back and he kisses her neck. It is a real long kiss just likes in the movies, and Grandma laughs as if her sides would split and her heart was going to break.

• • •

16
BRIDGES TO THE PAST

It seems to me that everyone who ever knew Grandma and Grandpa had sent them an anniversary card or telegram. It is my job to put these away. This is a very important job, says Mom. My sidekick, Cousin Howard, has gone back to California with Aunt Lily. I am on my own now, and I know exactly where the big yellow envelope marked "Golden Wedding" should go.

With a serious sense of purpose and great authority, I open the credenza drawer slightly and look inside. Room has to be made, that much is clear. The curious thing about the credenza drawer is that no matter how much stuff you take out of it, it always seems to be full.

My eyes dart this way and that. I cautiously avoid the awful death certificate. I take note of my mom's petrified sugar-cube corsage, and I place it behind a stack of old report cards bound by a rubber band. My gaze drops to the outside of the mahogany drawer where thick pewter rings extend defiantly out of the molded mouths of pewter lions. In an ongoing ritual, I pull the rings slowly, making the drawer slide open even farther. A vague yet comforting aroma drifts up from within, of pressed flowers, dry string, and old paper.

A quick once-over leads me to believe that the rear of the compartment, dark and hard to reach, is the best place for the big envelope. Fearing the drawer might get stuck, I clear away a packet of unused thank-you notes and a folder of bright cards from Mexico to add to my growing collection of picture postcards.

It is then that I first see them: a man and a woman. To all appearances, they are a couple, their images captured in the peculiar warm brown of photographs taken long ago. The man looks as stern as can be. The woman might as well have been dipped in starch. These are not people you would want to joke around with. They are fortunately stuck forever on that heavy cardboard. Gingerly, I lift the photo out of the drawer and study it. On the top right-hand corner, engraved into a fake ornate border, are the words: *Fotografie d'Arte.* I turn the "photograph of art" over.

There, in the faded blue ink of a bygone fountain pen, is the most beautiful handwriting I have ever seen. Sweeping curves and curlicues spell out words foreign and exotic.

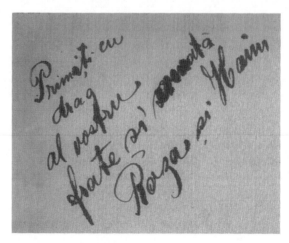

The note is signed with a flourish: *Roza si Haim*. This was Grandma's brother and his wife, my great-uncle and aunt.

That night I show the picture to Grandpa.

I turn the photo over so that he can see the fancy handwriting on the back. We look at it together, and I read out loud:

Prim-it-coo-drageh

"Tell me, Grandpa, what does it mean?"

"Prim-eat coo draga," he said, correcting my pronunciation. "Drag-A ... you pronounce it like when you say 'About.'

"But what does it mean?" I ask again.

"It means, *I send to you with affection.* Haim, he was my buddy, you know."

Grandpa tells a story I have heard before but cannot get enough of. It is all about how he and Haim became friends while serving in the Romanian Army, and how he had come home with Haim for a week's visit.

"How do you say it," Grandpa went on. "We were on ... LEAVE. That's it! You know, I was engaged to be married, to a cousin. I didn't love her, and I broke it off. Here I was, a single man, with my friend Haim.

"I saw your grandmother, and I liked her right away. Lively with pretty blue eyes, and she had a good figure." He smiled. "Then the matchmaker came to the house, trying to fix her up. But Grandma, she was independent! She said 'no' to this one and 'no' to that one. But with me she sat on the back porch and talked into the night, even when the moon was up. Her mother was a good, good lady but old-fashioned. She would say to Grandma, 'I don't understand it. What do you and Aba talk about so long on the porch?'

"I was in the house, in the parlor, when the matchmaker came again and gave Grandma one last chance. 'This is it!' she said. 'Enough is enough. The harness maker's son is not good enough, the tailor's son won't do. This is it. The shoemaker's son is the last boy I will bring to you,'" Grandpa chuckled. "I was getting ready to leave for the train station, to go back to Kishinev. Ha! Let me tell you, Jeffrey, you have to get up pretty early in the morning to put one over on me." He leaned forward and whispered to me. "So you know what I did?"

I shook my head "no." I had not heard this part before.

Reaching into his pants pocket, Grandpa takes out a round silver watch with a chain. I never saw anyone else who carried a watch like my Grandpa's. "A watch, just like this one," he said. "I left it behind *on purpose*. I went to the train station and I missed the train, *on purpose*. So I came back to see how the match turned out. Your Grandma, she said 'no' to the shoemaker's boy, and I stayed for an extra day, and then I came for a week, and then another week. And we talked and we talked on the porch in Iasi into the night, night after night." He laughed out loud. "And I came back again and again. And then, one night, on the porch, under the moon, when the lilac was out—oh, how I love the lilac." He pronounced it *lee-lak*. "When the lilac was out, that's when I proposed."

I didn't know it then but that photo of Haim and Roza, taken around World War I, would forge for me a firm and enduring bridge to the past. Out of its sepia depths, they stare at me. Uncle Haim with flashing eyes and handlebar mustache looks starchy in his three-piece suit and tie. Aunt Roza stands stiff in a dark tailored dress, a locket dangling from her neck. She gazes straight into the camera. "Say 'hello' to Uncle and me, time is passing," she seems to say. I could see why Grandma had "trouble" with her. I look at Haim and Roza so often and with such scrutiny that the sepia wallpaper behind them fairly quivers with color.

"What were Haim and Roza like, Grandma? What were they really like?
And Monis? And his wife?"

"Haim," Grandma said, "he looked like Uncle Mauritz, only taller. Haim and Monis were shoe manufacturers. Roza was a tailor's daughter. She dressed up all the time and thought she was something. Haim was in the Romanian Army with Grandpa. That's how we met. I was fussy about choosing boys, you know. The matchmaker had had it with me. 'Where do you think you are, Clara, Bucharest? Paree? One more chance, that's all!' Haim came home from the army for a week. He brought his friend Aba with him. Tall and straight and blond he was in that uniform, and so handsome. Quiet, but when he spoke you listened. When I saw him, I took Haim aside and I said: 'That is the kind of man I want.'"

Monis, the oldest brother, was a mystery. She spoke little of him. He was married, she said, yet she never uttered his wife's name.

"Monis had two girls and a boy," Grandma once divulged.

"How come there are no pictures?" I asked. "There are pictures of Haim and Roza."

"Monis had children," she replied. "He was too busy to take pictures. Haim didn't have children so he had time to take pictures."

Haim, it seemed, also had time to write. After my grandparents left for England, he and Grandpa corresponded faithfully.

My grandfather's brother Zeidel, also a cooper, had somehow landed a job in England. After a year or so, he wrote to Grandpa urging him to *come here and see what is going on here.*

My grandfather made the trip. This is 1901 and the British Empire is in its heyday. England is the place to be; "the center of the world" is what Grandpa called London.

Shortly afterward, he moved there with Grandma and baby Jack. He and Ziedel shared a small house, put the cooperage in the rear yard, and brought fellow coopers over from Romania to work. Cohen Brothers Coopers grew. My grandfather and his brother embraced England, prospered, and quarreled.

Almost a decade later, my grandparents would leave for America, their departure fueled by the fires of unspeakable tragedy. Grandpa never did as well here as in England. He had hoped, he once told me, to find work in the wineries of Northern California, but he ended up moored in Brooklyn and later the Bronx. Looking back, I expect his big move was from Balkan to Western Europe. He was hard working and loyal, industrious and clever, and no one ever messed with him. But he was, I suspect, too continental, too devoted to the wine cellar and cabaret, as he put it, too Romanian for rough-and-tumble America.

My grandparents last heard from Haim in 1925 with the arrival of his oft-quoted *mamaya morit* (mother has died) letter. On that mournful note, ties to our Romanian family seemed to dissolve…until World War II. As Europe went up in flames and anti-Semitism savaged the Continent like a wildfire, the ghosts of my great-uncles and their families would come back to haunt us, their fate an object of vast concern.

After the War, Grandpa and Uncle Mauritz, I am told, registered with HIAS, an agency dedicated to finding displaced Jews in Europe. But Romania, locked behind the Iron Curtain, did not yield its sad secrets easily. Haim and Roza and Monis and his wife and children drifted further and further into obscurity, like the land they came from. Except in the bedtime of my boyhood when my grandmother's voice, soft but urgent, gave them life. With time, the sound of her voice grew dimmer and dimmer, till it faded away altogether.

• • •

Part Two
THE SEARCH

17
FOOD FOR
THOUGHT

B y the 1970s, our family seemed to fall away. At first I thought that my grandparents, long gone, were the glue that had held us together. Perhaps it was simply that the world had changed. My cousins married and moved elsewhere. Older family members, present and obscure, faded from life. That which constituted "us" changed. My stepfather's family, vivacious and embracing, stepped in to fill the widening familial void.

As for me, after a boyhood of dreams, I fled Brooklyn for Manhattan to enter the land of the starving artist. Juggling alternate careers as fledgling actor, aspiring writer, and young filmmaker, I emerged finally as a freelance copywriter. Specializing in film and entertainment I wrote for publishers and cable stations, abridged novels for audio and, ever hopeful, peddled film scripts on the side. The pitfalls of freelancing and life on the go left little room for looking backward. I thought neither of the Old Country nor of a family I didn't really know or care about, or a past that might as well have been shrouded in dust. My only reminders of Romania were occasional, lively dinners with my Uncle Mauritz and Aunt Rae.

Food, I would find out, has exceptional powers. It can fuel time travel, cement generations, and even make pals of perfect strangers. To most of the family, and even in our house, Romanian cookery remains unknown. By the time I came along, my grandmother's cooking had become Americanized through her daughters and daughters-in-law, and Romanian dishes are prepared only for Grandpa.

While my mother and I eat southern fried chicken and sweet potatoes, Grandpa downs dishes drawn from the table of memory, strange concoctions that are further suspect to our sanitized taste buds. What haunts me most is an ungodly looking dish: a small anemic chunk of boiled fish at the bottom of a soup plate, trapped under the transparent quivering glaze of a nameless aspic. This, and the rest of Grandpa's meals, is finished off by hot red peppers, real scorchers that make him break out in a sweat.

In truth the ten years my grandparents spent in England left them with British accents and a perceived cultural distance from Balkan Europe. Uncle Mauritz and Aunt Rae maintain firmer ties to things Romanian. For one thing they came directly here from there. They are also considerably younger than Grandma and Grandpa, and more modern in every way—except when it comes to food. Mauritz, who had been a cook in the Romanian Army, never lost his passion for the national cuisine or for setting a continental table. Aunt Rae points to a dish of red roots shaved to look like flowers. "See what Uncle does," she says. "From radishes he makes roses."

I stand in their small dining room looking at a lace tablecloth on a lavishly set table. From the kitchen, a seductive aroma sails in on a sea of steam and spice. "Karnatztzlech" Grandma whispers with a warm smile, as Mauritz enters the room bearing a platter of zingy little sausages, just off the grill and bursting with buds of garlic. Big bowls follow: toasted buckwheat groats or *kasha*, thought of as "Jewish" in this country but a basic food eaten throughout Eastern Europe; smoky green *putlagela*, or *vinite*, a paste of oven-roasted eggplant mashed with a dash of olive oil, lemon juice, and sprinkled with grated raw onion, and a small serving of chopped red pepper or pine nuts at the cook's discretion; and finally, the dish of dishes: *mamaliga*.

• • •

Mamaliga is to Romania what pasta is to Italy, a national staple, eaten morning, noon, and night, hot or cold, and with a variety of accompaniments, depending on the region. It is essentially Romanian polenta, cooked in a pot, then turned upside down upon serving so that the great puff of cornmeal retains the shape of the pot bottom.

"Today, I will make a mamaliga," Grandma said, wiping her face with her apron. "We go to Dilbert's," she said. "We buy the cornmeal." She opens the clothes closet in the foyer and takes out my corduroy parka and her hand-me-down mouton coat. Then she ties a kerchief under her chin, as if to announce to the world: *I am from Europe.* I follow out the door as she leads the way, her dark-stocking bandy legs in old-lady shoes keeping a surprisingly brisk pace.

Down the block we go, and round the corner to the small mini-market. In the door, up to the counter, and it is all over.

"Hya, Mom," the big Italian guy behind the counter says. "What can we do for you today, sweetheart?"

"Just a nice head of green lettuce, Georgie."

Then to me, under her breath, as if reading my mind: "No mamaliga."

And so it goes. In our house mamaliga, applauded in story and song, never manages to make it to the kitchen table.

Why don't you ever make mamaliga, Grandma? You talk about it but you never make it!

The corn, the meal, isn't the same here. Not like in Romania.

She always said that, and I never question it until I start shopping and cooking for myself. Yellow cornmeal is yellow cornmeal, whether grown in the American heartland or the wheat fields of Romania. Stone ground is stone ground, no matter the continent.

Years later at a dinner table in Iasi, I would find the truth, that where Grandma came from even a simple task like making cornmeal mush was informed by legend and ritual. Which is not to say that I didn't get to enjoy a good mamaliga.

Grandma might have found making mamaliga in America disheartening, but that didn't stop Uncle Mauritz. While he fusses in the kitchen of that small apartment, we sit at the dining room table nibbling plump olives and celery stalks. Aunt Rae, theatrical as ever, preens while salting a radish, then bites into it with a crunch. Eyeing Grandma, she proceeds to enquire eagerly into my mother's love life.

Mauritz enters once again, bearing a ceramic platter with a proud mountain of yellow meal, and looking like the king of presentation.

"Mamaliga!" he announces.

"So thick that in the Old Country we cut it with a cord," said Aunt Rae.

"We ate it with Bryndza (sheep cheese)," Grandma adds.

Even after my grandparents were gone, the banquets continued, and I remained at least gastronomically Romanian, thanks to my aunt and uncle. But I would soon discover that my Balkan roots ran deeper than a nostalgic family meal.

• • •

18
IMAGINING THE PAST

1994: a small article in *The New York Times* advises that the Red Cross has accessed previously unavailable records of millions of Eastern Europeans imprisoned, or conscripted into forced labor, by the Third Reich. At the end of the article, I read that the Red Cross is also conducting family searches, and my interest is mildly piqued. I am, if nothing else, a sucker for any thing ripe with drama, especially related to World War II. Slowly, an idea is born.

I remember hearing that Grandpa and Uncle Mauritz registered with HIAS after the War to see if word had surfaced about our relatives over there, but nothing ever came of it. I think about it and think about it.

Now after years of silence, these forgotten ancestors make their presence known. I sense the tread of footsteps behind me. I hear muted whispers in a foreign tongue. Something indefinable fills the air, a mingled scent of pipe tobacco and stale perfume. Now Haim and Roza peer over my shoulder, along with Great-Grandma Sura and in the distance, so far off that I cannot make them out, Monis and his wife and children.

What happened to your brothers, Grandma? The brothers you left behind?

"Probably they were murdered," she said, as calmly as if she were balancing a bank statement.

The question was posed at the kitchen table, one quiet afternoon. I had just come home from school, and we had been studying World War II. We talked about the Jews and how terrible it was in Germany, in Poland, in the Netherlands, and in France. Nobody mentioned Romania.

Over the years, I realized that several possible circumstances might have defined our family's fate over there. Grandma's European brothers and sisters-in-law were older than she. They would have been on in years at the outbreak of The War. They might have died of natural causes before it happened, escaped or survived, or emigrated elsewhere between the two World Wars. They might have been destroyed by the havoc of the Holocaust or ended up God-knows-where in the colossal upheaval and displacement that followed.

Haim and Roza did not have children. But Monis had children, of whom I knew less than nothing, just that there were two girls and a boy. Unknown as these cousins were, they would have been relatively young in the 1940s. Perhaps they, or their children, or their children's children were alive … somewhere. The thing of it was that in all her tales of the Old Country, in all her family reminiscences, despite her penchant for detail and verbal embroidery, Grandma never mentioned the names of her oldest brother's children or that of his wife.

She spoke more of relatives who should have been supporting players on our family stage, like lively Aunt Leah and zany cousin Zasu or little Chaimerel, who unexpectedly split for Argentina. I could practically visualize Uncle Victor and the beer garden he ran in the Copou Park where Grandma and Grandpa seemed to go with their crowd. I knew a great deal about Haim and Roza and even Great-Grandma Sura. Surviving photos show her perpetually wrapped in a dark shawl and looking sour, the visual opposite of her reputation as a charitable, pious, and fondly remembered woman. "She was probably afraid of the camera," Mother said. "They all were in those days."

Grandma would describe her father, Great-Grandpa Hirsicu, in loving detail: how he worked as a miller, and the pleasure he took in going to the Turkish baths. She would often recall his untimely end, how he fell suddenly ill, asked Chaimerel to light his *trabuc*, and even as he waited for the doctor, took a big legendary puff on what would be his final cigar. So revered was he, Grandma said, that neighboring peasants came to the house, forming a long line at the door to pay respects to the widowed Sura and moneys owed her late husband.

Grandma drew vivid pictures of everyone except for her oldest brother and his family. All she ever said, with affection, was "My Monis…" and then her voice would trail off. I hadn't the foggiest notion of why, and it never occurred to me, as a young boy, to give it a second thought, no less ask questions.

Now, by the light of the Red Cross article, my lost European relatives begin to stir softly in the genetic recesses of my heart. Who was Monis? I seem to *know* that Monis manufactured shoes, just like Haim. But I know nothing when it comes to his wife or his children. Even as theories and possibilities percolate on the back burner of my mind, a dream occurs, an extraordinary dream, stunning in its simplicity, revelatory and far-reaching in consequence.

My grandmother, gone for decades, sits on a spindly wooden chair in a vacant room with walls painted the color of fog. She wears a black dress adorned by what used to be called "a drape," a swirl of cloth, sidelong from waist to hem. A familiar hat completes her outfit, the pillbox with the sequined autumn leaves she would wear to synagogue on the High Holy Days. In the dream, she looks at me with blue-grey eyes that are uncharacteristically devoid of emotion. Our conversation is brief.

What were the names of your nieces and nephews in Romania, of Monis's children?
I ask.

Corneliu. Adria. Gia, she murmurs.

With that, she is gone.

So vivid is the dream, so real, that I sit up in bed in utter amazement and hear
myself saying aloud: *Is my grandmother dead or alive?*

I call my mother the next morning.

"What do you know about Monis's children? Do you know their names? Did
Grandma ever tell you?"

"Why do you ask?

"Just tell me."

"Come to think of it, I don't know anything. Just that there were three. A boy and
two girls."

Three lost cousins. My grandmother never revealed their names in life, but
speaks them clearly in death. I want to know who they are, or were. First, to estab-
lish their identities as a point of departure for tracing them or their descendants
and, in my hearts of hearts, to know if something paranormal has happened. Did
Grandma pay a visit from the other side? A friend of mine versed in dream interpre-
tation adds more fat to the fire. Your grandmother is the link to the past, she says.
She wants you to find these people.

I register with the Red Cross. As I fill out the forms, it occurs to me: what do I
know about my great-uncles? Very little, it would seem. Two brothers. Shoe manufacturers, I believe. Both born in Stefanesti. Lived in Iasi. According to Grandma,
after her father died her older brothers packed the family up and left little Stefanesti
for the more cosmopolitan opportunities of Iasi, second largest city in the land.

I figure out their approximate years of birth. Haim had to be about as old as my
grandfather, since they both served in the Romanian Army at the same time. Monis
was the oldest and based on the age of Sura (his mother), he could have been as
much as ten years older than Grandma. Woefully little to go on, or so I thought.

At the same time, I join Rom-Sig, a Romanian-Jewish genealogy website group,
one of several specialty offshoots affiliated with Jewishgen.org. Through the group I
hire a researcher, Dr. Ladislau Gyemant, hoping he will draft a family tree. I expect
hardly anything to be found from a village as small and obscure as Stefanesti, but
I am fully prepared for success in Iasi, where Monis's children ought to have been
born and records are sure to have been kept.

Coincidentally Cousin Norman is in touch with me. He has been to London
where he had hoped to get a copy of Aunt Betty's (his mother's) birth certificate.
Instead he uncovered something of invaluable interest ... and not a moment
too soon.

We had all assumed that Grandma's maiden name was Neistadt, the surname
of her younger brother, Mauritz, my one great-uncle in America. It had crossed my
mind that Neistadt did not sound Romanian. But Jews, for one reason or another,
often had Germanic-sounding last names. Norman did not find his mother's birth
certificate but did obtain a copy of a birth certificate for little Goldie. On the certificate, Grandma's maiden name is listed as Grisar.

I am about to call my mother to tell her about this latest nugget when something comes to mind. Years back I needed a copy of my birth certificate. Mom told me to look in a binder on the top shelf of her bedroom closet.

That binder is packed with papers, and I proceed to rifle through reams of boring insurance policies and warranties. Finally I find what I am looking for, but peeking out from under my birth certificate is a document that appears to be antique. Gingerly I unearth a very old page of linen filled with mysterious words. Romanian words, penned in purple ink. At the top is the date: December, 1900. On the bottom there is what appears to be an official seal.

Mother says that this was Grandma's marriage certificate. Certainly there are signatures on the page, signatures I did not pay attention to at the time. Now I ask Mom to see the certificate.

Time has taken its toll and the edges of the fragile linen are crumbling. Yet the writing is still clear. A friend of mine who works with a Romanian born woman asks her to translate the piece for me. As it turns out, this is not a marriage certificate.

It is a dowry agreement and it states that the bride's mother is turning over a sum of 100 lei to the couple to be used for the sole purpose of setting up house. I pay careful attention to the signatures. Grandma's maiden name, signed by someone else, is hardly Neistadt and not Grisar but Grisariu.

Cousin Sylvia later explains that when her father came through Ellis Island, an immigration officer changed his last name to Neistadt. How Neistadt was chosen as Mauritz's new last name is anyone's guess, but the surname is a fiction. Sylvia tells me that her father fumed over it for years.

"Stupid Americans couldn't make out my name," Mauritz would rant, over and over, in spite of the fact that he had, so he said, a birth certificate signed by King Carol. I am certain the king had better things to do with his time, but my uncle claimed otherwise. Maybe it was rubber-stamped. Maybe an official representative did the honors. Maybe, for all I knew, Uncle Mauritz was right.

In any case, the very same name, Grisariu, had bedeviled the British official who executed Goldie's papers, and who transcribed it incorrectly as Grisar.

I pass the crucial information on to Professor Gyemant and not a moment too soon. He has started his good work, and within a month or two, our family tree arrives in the mail. It is packed with surprises.

Here an ample roster of departed ancestors reveals names long hidden in our foreign past. Lupu Grisariu. Henicu. Berticu. Cunea. Even a Maria or two. All were unknown to us. All born and lived and died from the late 1800s to the early 1900s, in Stefanesti. Occupations are listed, as are dates of birth, marriage, and death.

Then comes the prize of prizes, and a transforming snippet of paper: Haim Grisariu's birth certificate, translated from the Romanian by Dr. Gyemant. I just about go through the roof.

My great-uncle's birth certificate propels him out of the kingdom of fable into the arena of real life. Elaborate script, photocopied, bears witness to the birth of my grandmother's older, middle brother, *born on January 20, 1875, at 3 p.m.* This lost scrap of paper not only validates Haim's birth and very existence, but it also paints a picture of long-gone village life.

Great-Grandpa Hirsicu, it says, brought his new son to the town hall to be registered. "The Baby," the certificate goes on, "was born the day before yesterday in the house of his parents on Bacaului Strada." Based on signatures, Hirsicu's good friends Herscu Gansariu and Marcu Mazilu bore witness to the joyous event. Both worked as carters, while the registrar, Iconomu Necula, also doubled as mayor of the town. People kept busy in Stefanesti, it appears.

Nothing is as I expect. Whereas Professor Gyemant strikes gold in little out-of-the-way Stefanesti, he draws a blank in big-city Iasi, where Monis's children should have been born. A place where, one would think, records ought to have been kept.

Other surprises lay buried within the roots of our family tree, waiting to be discovered, and surfacing unpredictably. I had been told that Hirsicu was a miller. Ironically, the name "Grisariu" translates loosely from the Romanian as "miller." However, my great-grandfather is listed twice in the tree. Once, as *Hirsicu Grisariu, a servant,* and father of Haim. Fifteen years later he is listed again, as *Hirsicu A. Grisariu, a miller.* Evidently, Hirsicu had become so elevated in station that he now used his middle initial, thereby mistaken by the researcher as a different person.

Hirsicu A. Grisariu, occupation miller, is the father of the newly born Mauritz Iancu. Furthermore, Uncle Mauritz's middle name is to honor the memory of a preceding brother, Iancu, who apparently died in infancy. A shiver of sadness and pride run through me. I have connected through the years with a baby uncle whose short life has been long forgotten.

Monis remains a mystery, his presence conspicuously absent on the tree. Come to think of it, Grandma is nowhere to be found either. There is no record of birth for either of them. Did Monis come into this world in another town? Or, since he was the oldest, was he born in rural Stefanesti before births were recorded? What about Grandma? All I can think of is that perhaps she didn't rate a birth certificate because she was a girl.

Answers wait for me, I am certain, not in the Romania of my heart and mind, but on its distant, fabulous soil. In Iasi. In Stefanesti. In dusty archives. On crumbling tombstones. Perhaps in the stories of old people left behind. Somewhere in Romania family ghosts wait ready to shed unearthly light on our murky Balkan past.

For years, independent travel in Romania had been difficult. But this is 1995, and the country has been open to the world since 1989 when the Romanian Revolution overthrew a ruthlessly repressive Communist regime. I think about it carefully. Iasi and Stefanesti, the places my grandparents reminisced about. Bucharest, the capital they spoke of in awe and where Uncle Mauritz, young and dashing and eligible, spent a night on his way to Paris with two bachelor pals.

These were the places of our past, ancestral cities, towns, and regions waiting to be explored, felt, tasted, inhaled, experienced. Although I am used to traveling solo, going to Eastern Europe alone seems daunting. I covet company, and on such a trip as this, who could be a more appropriate companion than my mother.

I envision us walking across the Red Bridge where Grandma and her friends once gossiped and joked, strolled, and flirted. Perhaps we would find her house in Iasi, where lilacs might still bloom on the backyard porch or see the primary school in Stefanesti, an esteemed place whose proud classrooms my grandmother never knew. Certainly we would visit the cemetery where Hirsicu and Sura, maybe Haim and Roza, sleep undisturbed by visitors for decades. At the very most, we might find something meaningful, tangible, or revelatory about our missing relatives. At the very least, we will see where we come from.

We had cash. We had courage. All we needed was a connection. Well, this is New York. Within weeks, a friend who knows a friend put me in touch with one Bruno Blumenthal, who lives not far from me and had gone to college in Iasi. I will soon find out that if you are in Romania, going to college in Iasi is not as unusual as it might seem.

My relationship with Bruno is confined to the telephone. He is cordial, good-humored, and eager to help. Best of all, he has a contact for us. Vonda Condurache. "Does Vonda Condurache sound like a Jewish girl to you?" Bruno asks, laughing. In fact, Vonda is one of the few young Jews left in Romania, and she is a journalist for TV-Iasi. I am sure her ethnic and professional background will be of immeasurable value in researching synagogue records, exploring the countryside around Iasi, and even getting to Stefanesti, which appears on the map to be two full fingers away from Iasi. I write to Vonda, a careful cordial letter introducing myself and telling her of our plans.

Within a week, I am awakened at five in the morning by the whir of my fax machine. I am totally perplexed. Who could be faxing me at such an ungodly hour? The place of origin tells all. This is my first fax from overseas, a matter-of-fact but extremely warm hello from Vonda Condurache: our "woman in Romania."

• • •

19
CONSIDERING ROMANIA

Swinging into action, the first thing to do is to gather family documents, and I call Cousin Sylvia to see if Uncle Mauritz had left any "official" papers behind. Copies of his birth certificate and Romanian Army papers are still around, she says, complete with a description of the young Mauritz, not my silver-haired uncle but a dashing lad with copa (brown) eyes and negru (black) hair. Best of all, the papers show addresses of where the family had lived both in Iasi and Stefanesti.

Next I head straight for the old credenza, which has tailed my mother from Brooklyn to Manhattan. Pinned against a wall in a long foyer the credenza no longer occupies a central position in her household, and its mahogany finish has been lacquered black, victim of a do-it-yourself redecorating fad.

Some things do change. No longer a naive boy, I open the credenza drawer, once dreaded, without hesitation. Haim and Roza's faces stare back at me still, with a keen sense of beckoning. Time, however, has not diminished the appetite and capacity of the drawer to collect and store memorabilia, and it has given birth to a whole new generation of paperwork and pictures. Here, my stepfather's discharge papers from World War II; there a sepia photo of my mother, age ten or so, on a horse; and a series of recent and undistinguished snapshots of relatives on both sides.

Slowly, deliberately, sensing that something of value might surface, I move my stepfather's army papers aside to reveal a cluster of short stories from my mother's high-school yearbook. Under those white paper sheets lay a much older, yellowing document, obviously an "official" text of some kind. I lift the high-school clippings to take a closer look. It is the death certificate from London. I have not thought of it in years. I have not looked at it since that day when my Cousin Howard and I, both implausibly young, happened upon it.

The last time I saw the certificate, I had shoved it back to the rear of the drawer. Young and impressionable and possessed by panic, I had never examined the document in its entirety. Removing it from the drawer slowly, I look at it with the jaundiced eye of an adult who understands that death happens.

I read again that description of the cause of death, poetic in a chilling way: "Violent burns and shock ... while dusting the mantelpiece looking glass." I remember now. My eyes travel up the page, to the line just above the cause of death, where the name of the deceased appears. A telltale name that jumps off the page and fairly rocks the room: *Yetta Cohen*. Not *Goldie*. I read on in disbelief: *32 years of age, wife of Zeidel, a cooper*. I call my mother to the credenza and show her the certificate.

"I thought this was Goldie's."

"No. This death certificate was for Yetta. She was Zeidel's wife. They stayed on in London."

My mother doesn't seem to realize the implications of what had happened so many years ago. Two family members, child and adult, aunt and great-aunt, had perished by fire, possibly in the same fireplace, and a scant year apart. Shocking tragedies aside, the sheer chance of it was Dickensian in scope, a story screaming to be told.

"What happened after?" I ask.

"Zeidel came here with his children. He remarried but he died a couple of years later."

"His children?"

"Yes. Benny. And Annie."

"Annie Dinkles!"

"That's right. And the youngest was Joseph... who became Gentleman Jim."

"Were there any others?"

"Another boy. Davy."

I was floored. I had never pieced together the relationships. I knew that Gentleman Jim and Annie were orphaned and had lived for a while with my grandparents when my mother was a little girl, but I never made the connections.

"Zeidel remarried?...." I am looking for answers, and Mother finishes my sentence for me.

"She was a good woman, but she couldn't afford to support four children, so they were put into an orphanage for a while until it was decided what could be done. The boys came to live with us. Annie went to Tante ChaRussa, Grandpa's sister. But later she came to us too."

My mother then tells me that Davy and Gentleman Jim both ran away from home when they were teenagers. Benny, she said was a prizefighter.

"A prizefighter!"

"Yes. You know, I can't figure out where they slept. There was hardly enough room for us."

• • •

20
TOURISTS

I have no idea of what to expect in Eastern Europe, but three months later we are on our way. Hoping for the best yet expecting the worst, I decide to start off in cities with solid tourist credentials, chain hotels, and the like, names well known in the West. A given, or so I thought, was that neither my mother nor I would be likely to visit this part of the world again—or at least anytime soon. Our ambitious yet sensible itinerary begins with brief stays in Prague and Budapest followed by rail travel into Romania.

In Prague we drink coffee in the square where once Kafka lingered, and take lunch in the café Melina named after his mistress. We watch as puppeteers make colorful puppets dance along the cobbled stones of the King Charles Bridge, and we visit the 13th century synagogue in Old Prague. In its cemetery, weathered aged tombstones seem to sink into the misty past. Our hotel, hardly a chain item, is an exercise in continental polish. Its plush lobby is prelude to a room warmed by rich mahogany armoires. Gracious chandeliers and fringed window shades are cordial mementoes of bygone splendor.

On our second day in Prague, we promenade down elegant avenues lined with original, absolutely perfect Art Nouveau buildings. Why such pristine preservation here when other large cities in Europe were ravaged by World War II? What special privilege enabled architecturally splendid Prague to evade the ruin that befell Warsaw or Leningrad, or even London?

The answer lies not in an appreciation of building style but an endorsement of the perverse. Hitler, we are told, spared the Czech capital in what could only be deemed a grotesque flourish to his final solution of the Jewish problem, a notion that one might call the final insult. There was, as always, a maniacal method to Hitler's madness.

Der Fuehrer kept Prague out of harm's way so that its lovely buildings would one day showcase looted Judaica: menorahs and torahs stripped from synagogues throughout Europe; ceremonial plates and goblets stolen from homes where once Jews lived; prayer shawls and books of psalms wrenched off the backs and out of the hearts of the devout. In a continent cleansed of Jewry, Hitler's Prague would draw visitors from far and wide, to view what he shockingly foresaw as the pride of the Reich. A cruel monument to murdered Jews, his Prague would become what he called the "Museum of a Vanished Race."

• • •

We fly to Budapest via Magyar Airlines and find the Hungarian capital to be a heady, if unlikely, alliance of economic confidence and geographic mystery. Architecturally Budapest is an eclectic revelation: one knows one is not in the West. Glitzy shops crackle with a sense of fashion and contemporary achievement while grand thoroughfares and aged stone buildings glorify past grandeur.

On a tourist ferry, we sail up the Danube and under the seven bridges that connect hilly downtown Buda with the charming flatlands of residential Pest. In Buda, we sip Tokay wine in small cafes, and stroll along a tiled waterside esplanade, eyeing others who have apparently come to be seen. Just across the river, in Pest, small shops and green gardens enhance a splendidly restored medieval castle; orange-tiled rooftops slumber in the Hungarian sun; breathtaking city views beckon from balconies on Castle Hill; and behind spires on Old Town rooftops.

We tour the baroque Basilica of St. Stephen, overshadowed by its vaulted ceilings and lifelike statuary. We visit the Grand Synagogue where Moorish columns pierce the heavens. We are told it is the largest temple in Europe, and caters to what appears to be a remarkably intact Jewish community.

Wartime Budapest suffered a fate quite unlike that of Prague. Unwilling to compromise its famed sophistication, the Hungarian capital managed to maintain an aura of prewar gaiety even as the world around it crumbled. But in the end it proved a fragile shield against Nazi wrath. Despite heroic political efforts, the axe fell at the eleventh hour and Jews were arrested and deported to Auschwitz with bullet fire speed. In that most infamous and efficient death camp, twelve thousand Hungarian Jews a day were gassed without even the customary selection process.

A photo exhibit in the gallery of the synagogue depicts deportation and arrival. Out of the grim past, Hungarian Jews stand in trackside muck, gazing out at camp and camera in disbelief. Women with kerchiefs wrapped around their foreheads, peasant-style, some with babes in arms stand near mustachioed men in berets or fedoras, faces frozen with fear and shock.

Boys in caps bear expressions of concern beyond their years. Sweet girls, faces framed by long taffy colored braids, are visibly upset. Twin brothers, all dressed up in fur-lined ethnic capes and jaunty little hats appear puzzled. Others, creeping out of dusty cattle cars, gaze upon a sea of yellow Stars of David, their eyes filled with hurt and distrust.

MYSTERIOUS PLACES

• • •

21
FOREIGN INTRIGUE

We take the night train out of Hungary, my mother and I, bound for Romania on the ten-hour route from Budapest to Bucharest. At seventy-five, my mother is petite, still attractive, and energetic. Although she bills herself, justifiably, as the original working mother, Mom is part of that generation of Jewish-American women who turned housekeeping into a religious experience.

In my mother's case, cleanliness is next to chic. She is if nothing else well turned-out, and three days in fashionable Budapest leaves a dreamy smile on her face that is dissolved by hours of riding the rails through limitless Hungarian plains and tawny thatched-roofed towns. We say nothing, prisoners of this seedy train, wheels grinding endlessly along unknown tracks through the middle of nowhere.

Suddenly the car screeches to a halt, causing Mom and I to lurch forward. We reclaim our respective spaces, and I look once again into her eyes. She stares back, calm yet concerned, while repeatedly smoothing out the hem of her slate grey skirt, trying to bring order to uncertainty. As if to commiserate, the train lets out a giant mechanical wheeze and the lights begin to flicker. Mother casts a puzzled glance my way before an unexpected blanket of darkness erases her face. "Oh my God," I think, considering the possibilities. "What have I done?"

In the next car, an iridescent light twinkles nervously like a wand in the dark. I rise to take a step or two. Peering into gloom and squinting hard, I am able to make out the source of light. Two cigarettes, waved about by a soldier and his girl, brighten the shadows like a firefly's glow on a dark summer night. I would like to approach the couple to see if they know what has happened, but my instincts scream "do not take that step." I am certain that should I enter their car and dare strike up a conversation, I will never be heard from again. The entire setting shrieks "foreign intrigue."

Our destination is Timisoara, Romania's largest westernmost city situated on Lake Timis in the neighborhood of Hungary. According to the train schedule, we have barely three minutes to disembark, and our surly conductor says some cars will soon be detached. But he won't say which cars, or when, nor will he tell us if the lights will ever go on again. All queries are answered in two little words, which seem to be universal English in this part of the world: *no problem.*

In my worst daydreams, I struggle with luggage for two on a station platform as the three-minute deadline dissolves in the engine's shrill whistle. There I stand, a lone American near the wilds of the Hungarian/Romanian border, watching the train charge off into the horizon carrying with it my mother, innocent victim of unintended sabotage.

I devise a contingency plan. If we are separated, I tell Mother she is to ride to the end of the line, last stop Bucharest, and check into the Inter-Continental Hotel where we have reservations. I will follow on the next train. "Don't worry," she says. "Everything will be alright once we are in Romania." I am about to learn something on this trip: *Mother knows best . . .* and she is not without her charms.

"Anyway," she adds, "we are almost there." I ask her how she knows this, and she answers that she has overheard someone mention the word *granitz*, which is evidently pan-European lingo for *border.* Mother knows this from a story Grandpa used to tell that reached its third act with the curtain line, "when we got to the *granitz*" (the border crossing).

The granitz factor, as it turns out, is a point of conjecture that had been discussed at length with friends in New York before leaving. We wondered how the Romanian authorities would handle passport inspection as we are slated to pull into the granitz at three in the morning. My friend Ed comes up with the most sensible solution. Since no one can get on or off the train, he figures, passports will be inspected once we reach the first stop in Romania at a more reasonable hour. "That's it!" I agree. "They're not going to wake everyone up in the middle of the night!"

That, as it turns out, is exactly what happens. At three in the morning, the compartment door swings open and a big cannonball of a Madame, seemingly left over from Soviet days, stands in the doorway. In her drab olive uniform, a hand on each side of the door, she looks as if she is going to sing, or at least widen the doorway. Instead she stands there, a female Samson, demanding to see our passports while holding up the walls of the temple.

Shortly after dawn, the train chugs its way out of Hungary and into Romania proper, slowing to a halt at a whistle stop called Curtici. A surreal landscape greets us, enhanced by a trackside cafe that looks neither Eastern nor European but more like a rustic log cabin in the American Wild West.

Clattering heels announce the entrance of the authorities and a herd of navy blue uniforms appears out of nowhere. To my surprise, dispelling all stereotypes, these border officials are courteous and efficient, and their English is impeccable. One of the men, a tall and mustachioed officer approaches us, introducing himself as the "papers checker."

"He looks like Robert Taylor," my mother whispers, referring to a dashing movie idol of her Depression-era girlhood. "Robert Taylor" introduces a young woman whom he refers to as "the bank lady." Then he stands at attention with pride as the Bank Lady painlessly changes our Yankee money into Romanian currency. Once the transaction is done, Robert Taylor points to the café.

"You must take a juice or coffee," he says. "There is enough time," he adds, flashing a smile that could make him famous. Delighted, we go to the door of the train. A metal ladder, mercifully short in length, leads to the station floor. A closer look reveals that dismounting will require an athletic jump from last step to ground. I cast a look of alarm at my little Mom who measures in at just under five feet.

"My mother will never be able to do this," I plead with the Paper Checker aka Robert Taylor. Without reservation he sweeps Mom up in his arms and carries her from the train, down the ladder, and into the café. I follow into the dimly lit woodsy space just in time to see him place her on a counter stool. Mother, fairly glowing, smiles knowingly at me.

Comes departure time Robert Taylor magically reappears and, like all gallant young heroes, whisks mother into his arms once more and carries her off…or at least back to our train.

• • •

22
TIMISOARA

"*Do the trains run on time?*" I ask the agent at the Romanian Tourist Office in New York.

"*On time? On time? ... This is Romania.*"

We are due in Timisoara at 1 a.m. and we pull into the station at one on the button. We are on time! I had envisioned us creeping into a dark deserted place, but

Romania travels by rail and one in the morning at the station in Timisoara looks like nine at night in other American cities.

And what a station! Pink tiles lead to a majestic waiting room packed with travelers scurrying here and there. Everyone seems to be going somewhere, and shopping bags are the luggage of choice. These are gargantuan, overstuffed, chintzy affairs carted around by partners in transit, one person to a side, plastic handles straining at the bit.

I stop for a moment, trying to figure out how to get my mother and me out of here, but we are sinking in surreal quicksand. Too many signs point at too many archways, and each dissolves into what appear to be endless passageways. We stand there, wondering which way to go, noticed only by the walls...or so we think.

A hearty woman sees our confusion. She is lugging one of those bulky shopping bags with the help of a girl half her age. Much to her younger companion's surprise and unhappiness, the older woman drops the ungainly bag and approaches us. In pidgin Romanian, I ask for directions. I am answered by a stony onceover, etched in wonderment. A moment later, the woman looks at my mother, and a smile brightens her apple-cheeked face. Nodding, the big lady grabs Mom's suitcase and starts off, gesturing for us to follow. Overruling my objections and driven by purpose, she charges ahead, leaving the young girl behind to wrestle the giant shopping bag.

Trailblazer that she is, the big woman occasionally glances back to make sure we are still with her, then resumes her mission, leading us up and down and around shadowy staircases. Suddenly she stops short, and with abundant good will and obvious pride, she deposits us in the lobby near a taxi stand. Taking my mother's hands in hers, and eyeing me as well, the big woman smiles warmly.

"*Bine soarta* (good luck)," she whispers.

A moment of camaraderie warms the three of us, and then the big lady whirls around, reclaims her side of the giant shopping bag, and vanishes into the crowd, her petite young companion by her side.

Our young cab driver, Claudiu, turns out to be a second good friend and peerless guide. On our way to the hotel, his cab scoots down a long-dark-wide boulevard dwarfed by hulking buildings. Ornate terra cotta rooftops pierce the inky sky above. Weathered Gothic buildings recall those old apartment houses along New York's West End Avenue; imperious structures whose baroque entrances defy entry.

Claudiu seems to be reading my mind. In impeccable English, he advises that this part of Romania once belonged to the Hapsburg (Austro-Hungarian) Empire, a pedigree that in its palmy days caused Timisoara to be crowned "Little Vienna." Signs, newspapers, and café menus reveal an ongoing Hungarian and German presence.

Before saying goodbye, I tell Claudiu with pride why we are here. "My grandparents came to America from Romania many years ago," I explain.

"I will be leaving for Toronto soon," he responds with an engaging smile. The truth lies heavy in the night air between us. I have come to find my past in a country that, for many, does not yet hold a future.

Out of nowhere, light shines brightly out of the milky globe of an antique street lamp. On its face, illuminated black letters boldly proclaim that this was once "the first city in Europe to be lit by electricity." Claudiu tells us this was also the first city in what is now Romania, and the second city in all Europe, to reap the high speed of a horse-drawn tram. We drive past towering stucco walls framed by huge plants and a sign reading *sanitoria*. Mother leans over and whispers: "I'd hate to be put up in that place."

By the time we arrive at our hotel, the city is pitch dark. Making our way to the lobby, we pass several men who lean back lazily against a waist-high wall, cigarettes dangling out of their mouths. "Dolares," we hear one whisper to the other as we pass by. Much to my amazement, and dismay, we have been pegged as Americans without even speaking a word. Across the street, ancient buildings hide in the shadows; flickering street lamps offer fleeting glimpses of ornate multi-colored facades.

Shabby chic defines the lobby of our hotel. Walls are papered in Valentine red flock. Plastic greenery flowers out of shiny metal pots at the check-in counter, by elevator doors, and in random corners. It is late and the only visible patron is a middle-aged woman, sitting in a throne of a chair, hennaed hair and heavy makeup glistening under incandescent ceiling lamps. Our room turns out to be surprisingly comfy, though the peculiar gerry-rigged faucet in the tub inspires instant hilarity.

Next morning, we discover that the goofy deficits of décor and plumbing are more than offset by the glowing warmth of the staff. Leaving our room we are waylaid by a cheery chambermaid who specializes in breaking through the language barrier. Pantomime is the way and she does not hold back. She flutters. She gasps. She waves her eyebrows about like semaphores. Her message is clear: follow me.

Down the hall we go, after the merry maid, only to dead-end at a large curtained window framed by a blank off-white wall. Fairly dancing with excitement, the maid pulls back a cream-colored drape, and sunlight streams into the hall. With a sweep of the hand, she points with pride to a panorama of rolling ochre hills brushed by rows of tall deep green poplars. By night Timisoara had seemed dim and dusty as a naked bulb in a lonely room; by the light of day, it is as bright as a polished mirror and, we are about to find out, as lively as a silent movie comedy.

Breakfast consists of hearty helpings of hard rolls and bitter coffee. Fanta orange pop pinch-hits for OJ, and not just for the morning meal. You can buy that bubbly orange soda at all hours, in outdoor stalls, on street corners, and in case you should have a memory lapse, it is promoted in colorful print and paint on the sides of city buses. Charging down the avenue at madcap breakneck speeds, these vintage vehicles are jam-packed with passengers hanging out of open windows and pressed against doors. This is definitely not for Mom, and it is lucky we are within walking distance of the center city.

Not far from the screwball streetcars and gaudy Fanta signs, we discover Victoria Square, the elegant yet friendly heart of the city. A classic *corso*, or tiled concourse, runs its length, creating a sunlit, gardened plaza that inspires promenade. Two- and three-story buildings with curvilinear hooded roofs line the corso. Bronzed spires look skyward while slightly shuttered windows cast sidelong glances at glorious flowerbeds below. For all its baroque credentials, Timisoara is an architectural hybrid: unlikely yet beautiful child of Constantinople, Vienna, and Budapest; and fetching offspring of Turkey and Austria-Hungary.

This is the late '90s and Romania, on the heels of long and abusive Communist rule and recent revolution, still shifts uneasily at the bottom of the economic ladder. Yet political disaster has not dimmed the nation's legendary joie de vivre, and with its unexpected Mediterranean climate, this corner of the Bsnat encourages dining and wining al fresco.

Further down the corso, multicolored umbrellas spill welcome shade on intimate tables where patrons, often families, down velvety ice cream, drink thick coffee, or sip wine. In a small outdoor café across the way, we sit under an equally festive umbrella.

"Order me the mushroom," my mother says. "You speak more Romanian than I do."

"I'll be lucky if I can get two words understood," I respond.

The mushroom in question is the stuffing of choice in our first Romanian-style pizza ever—and what a pizza. Unlike its Italian (American) cousin, this is a feathery cream puff of a pie that rests airily on and obscures an unexpectedly thin crust. Toppings are generous but Romanians make you hunt for the cheese, and they do not kill their pizza with tomato sauce but serve it in a bowl on the side.

Later in the afternoon, we enjoy a glass of fruity Romanian wine, so often applauded at home by Grandpa and Uncle Mauritz. Cheeses are rich. Pastries are plenty, sausages spicy, yet mamaliga, to our disappointment, is nowhere to be found.

This wine is better than good, and good Americans that we are, we show our appreciation by stuffing money into the palms of our young waitress. "No, no," she cries, recoiling. After dinner, an attempt to tip our dark-haired waiter is greeted by a shy smile and a nod that says "no" less theatrically than the earlier waitress. Greed, it appears has not yet found a place in the Romanian vocabulary, or economy. I lean over to my mother. "Our new-world roots are showing," I whisper. "We are the ugly Americans."

At the head of Victoria Square, looking out over the corso in regal and intriguing splendor is the second version of the city's famous opera house. It took four years and a fleet of Viennese architects to engineer the original House built on swampland in 1875. "Legend has it," we are told, "that the original opera house stood firm on a thick base of 1,600 oak logs."

Later reading reveals that this is no legend but firm fact. Timisoara's glorious Piata Operei entered the 20th century in a blaze of fame, followed by fire that reduced it to ashes. Reincarnated in the 1920s, the building is a showcase of the lavish and melodramatic Neo-Byzantine architecture embraced by Jazz Age Romania.

Three Turkish arches frame a front balcony, intricately carved with detail that could only be called, well, operatic. From such a terrace could Onegin's Tatyana bare her lovelorn heart to the heavens, would Lucia di Lammermoor court madness to a lyrical moon, and Carmen toss a crimson rose to an overheated matador.

In front of these very arches, in such a place, did over one thousand Romanian soldiers lose their lives fighting in what was the first and only violent uprising against Communist rule. By day, the white opera house of Timisoara gleams like a diamond in the sun. By night, as if to celebrate uprising, its ivory walls catch fire in a blaze of orange light.

Inside, the opera house lobby, lined with gilded frescoes of Romanian folk and fairy tales, is as splendid as its exterior wrapping. No one is shy, and we are again recognized as foreigners. "We Romanians have always been, how do you say, excellent, at opera," a passerby informs us.

Timisoara may once have been called Little Vienna, but we soon find out why it is being touted today as the Romanian Prague. Exploring cobbled alleys and winding streets on our second day, we find the key to a city that reaches back beyond the days of Hapsburg glory. Restoration is apparent in colorfully painted facades of faded 13th century villas, ornately carved doorways, in curlicue columns and sculpted arches of stone buildings, and new lampposts in the antique fashion.

A fanciful pale green palace looks down on the Piata Unireii, its interior transformed into an art gallery. The city's continental heritage is apparent in the Serbian bishop's palace, in elaborate spires of the Serbian Orthodox Cathedral, and in the buttery yellow dome of Saint George's Roman Catholic Cathedral fronted by a fluted, soaring Votive obelisk.

At the Piata Unireii, we sit and reflect. Bullet marks scar the weathered brick walls of this ancient place, mute witness to recent history. This is where the spark that lit the Revolution of 1989 caught fire. This is where gunfire leads to riot and the execution of Nicolae Ceausescu and his wife, to the downfall of his reign of terror, and the return of Romania to the modern world.

Pigeons take flight, watched only by indifferent statues and two elderly women in kerchiefs. One speaks English and we talk briefly. "You heard?" she asks. "They shot the big one!"

"Yes, we know. The world knows. Things will be better." She shrugs. "They made a revolution," she says, "but they don't know what do with it"

• • •

23
TRANSYLVANIA

*D*ue *billete din Iasi*, I recite with great assurance to the station agent. She nods to me and we exchange smiles. I have been told that my pronunciation is flawless, and I am certainly well rehearsed. Without hesitation, the fare is quoted to me, and I am feeling utterly Romanian when a voice in back of me advises, in clipped English: "It is very cheap, isn't it!"

Busted again! Pegged once more as an American, this time by a dark-eyed student from Egypt, also headed for Iasi where he will go to medical school. From what he tells me Iasi, unknown to most westerners, is regarded in his part of the world as *the* place to study medicine. "There are many schools here," he says.

I rummage through my wallet to come up with the right amount. Even in America, I had no mind for numbers and now I am at a complete loss, especially given the mountain of tickets handed to me—more tickets I am sure than there are stations on our trip.

A man thrusts his stubby fingers under my nose. "Uno, due, tre" he says. Rifling through my unwelcome pile of tickets, he tries to explain how these relate to cost.

"I know, I know," I say, proud of the fact that I can count in Romanian. "One, two, three...."

Like football players in a huddle, the others in the room descend upon me, driven by the need to refine my ability to count in Romanian, and to make sure that I understand how to sift through and sort out the mountain of tickets. Hands gesture left and right glorying in the national penchant for dramatic excess. One can see why Romanians excel in opera.

At last we are aboard. It takes sixteen hours to cross the country from Timisoara, near the Banat and sandwiched between the Danube and the Carpathians, to northeastern Iasi, snuggled up against the Russian border. Our compartment has seen better days. Seats of blotchy patterned dull-green corduroy are comfortable but threadbare and occasionally patched.

First comes the Juice Man, a wiry old fellow with a small crate of bottles, a big mustache, and an even bigger smile. He is also a model of inefficiency. It will certainly take endless trips to fill and refill orders for juice as he makes his way up and down the long, long train. Either that or he doesn't expect to sell much. With boyish delight, the Juice Man asks in English: "Do you want a refreshment?" Once more we are instantly recognized as westerners. As I pay for our juices, he asks where we are going.

"To Iasi."

"Ooh, Iasi!" His face lights up.

Across from us sit a darkly handsome couple. They are young and in love and cannot keep their hands off each other. They bill and coo. They kiss and nuzzle. They feed each other nuts and raisins from a crumpled paper bag.

Now comes the Ticket Man. I still hold in my hand the gargantuan pile of tickets issued at the station, and it is his job to punch a hole in each ticket at every whistle stop, tiny town, and big city on the long voyage back to where once we came from.

"Americans?" the Ticket Man asks, in decent English. We've been spotted once again. His eyes open wide when we tell the Ticket Man we are from New York, and then he leaves in a hurry.

As the train rolls on, it is apparent at every station, large or small, that despite Romania's woes, public places are well kept as attention is paid to the way things look. Blossoming vines twine around every place sign, potted flowers bloom on every rail platform.

Between the Juice Man and the Ticket Man, word is out: foreigners are aboard, not just foreigners, but westerners, and not just westerners but Americans. People pop by and poke their heads in. Some say hello, some ask where we are going, and others gawk in silence, or pantomime a greeting. Even the conductor pays a visit.

"So few people come from the West!" he says. "Where are you going?"

"Iasi."

"Very nice, Iasi."

In this country, so long forgotten, and especially in this exotic neck of the woods, tourism is a rarity and we, the tourists, are accidental celebrities. Tourism means magic. Now and for the duration of our trip, more than one Romanian will express pride in the extravagant natural beauty of the country, and awareness that tourism could be the nation's ticket back to economic vitality.

The train chugs on, through mountain and flatland, bypassing an occasional castle, skirting stray clusters of huts, and into breathtakingly green, painfully exquisite countryside.

Our traveling companions change with the scenery. Seated next to the couple now is a woman, well into middle age and given to regal posturing. Perching on the edge of her seat as if riding sidesaddle, she tosses long grey hair about like silver lightning. Despite her simple floral dress, she assumes dignity with such effect that my mother and I nickname her "the Countess." Primping seems to come naturally to the Countess, and she finds our attention agreeable.

As the train engine revs up, a paunchy old man in suspenders barrels his way into the compartment. Barely fitting through the door, he squeezes in just in the nick of time. Born to amuse, his loud manner and boisterous jokes send everyone into gales of laughter, including Mom and me even though we do not understand a word.

I am impressed by how solicitous the young lovebirds are of my mother, a salute to seniority you would not find so quickly at home. Is she comfortable? Would she like some nuts and raisins? They mime, while holding the paper bag up in a gesture of offering. Does she know that a footrest extends from under the seat?

In an obvious response to inadequate interest on our part, the Countess heads for the corridor where she strikes an aristocratic pose by the window, giving her silvery mane a royal toss or two while casting sidelong glances our way.

At the next station, the old bozo rushes off. He is not yet back when the train engine revs up, and history repeats itself. Holding ice creams for everyone, he races against time across the platform to make the train. Suspenders bulging, big belly bouncing, he enters puffing to hearty applause. Ice cream is served, and the train rolls on.

We are making our way through the emerald forests of Transylvania. From out of the dense green treetops, one by one, wooden outposts emerge at regular intervals. Each of the roughhewn platforms bears a single young soldier. How proudly they stand, one more handsome than the next, chests held high, and hands behind backs. How strong and brave they look in their khaki shorts and shirts with tri-colored neckerchiefs in the yellow-and-black-and-red of the Romanian flag.

An hour or two later, our traveling companions are gone. Alone, we sit gazing at the splendid lush forest view when the train pulls in at a small town. A young father with two boys enters our compartment. He is an attractive man with an edge to him that prompts my mother to whisper to me that he looks like a rock star. Which he does. The Rock Star is too busy settling his kids to notice us, but his bright-eyed boys sure do.

"Didn't I tell you," my mother begins. And I know what she is about to say. During the 1970s, my mother and stepfather had gone on a trip to Romania. This was during the reign of the dictator Ceausescu, and it was a carefully guided tour. Her impression of the country was one of endlessly changing splendid scenery, and an adoring assessment of Romania's children, proven by the positively angelic demeanor of the Rock Star's sons.

"Didn't I tell you," mother says aloud, "Romanian children are the most beautiful in the world."

Overhearing this, the Rock Star smiles broadly. He understands English, speaks it well, and tells us he is taking the boys to see their grandparents. Florien, a brown-haired lad in a green parka, is perhaps 12. Sandy-haired Christian wears an identically styled parka, as blue as his sparkling eyes. He is no more than ten. Florien is instructed to practice his English with us. "How do you do?" he says with a faint, irresistible accent as he extends his hand.

We are riding through lush woods once again. The rock-star father, suddenly quiet, looks out at the remarkable greenery. Our gaze follows his. "Romania," he says, "it is beautiful." He looks out the window a moment longer, then turns back to face us.

"And then there is THIS!" he says in a low sad voice, pointing to the raggedy seat of the shabby train.

I look back at the passing forest again. This is no ordinary forest. This is the forest of Transylvania. Greener than green. Darker than dark. Seductive. Bewitching. Fearful. In such a place as this, jewel-like and primal, you could see how superstition could fire the heart and legends be born. Here the notion of the vampire would be spawned in stories destined to haunt the nights of the world. From these leafy, shadowy woods, in this unearthly corner of the Earth, would Romania be molded into a land weaned on myth.

Twilight colors the sky purple and the train rolls slowly toward Moldavia. What, I wonder, will we find in Iasi, this city that once was ours.

• • •

24
IASI

Mist veils the station in Iasi. It is barely 9:30 at night when the train pulls in, yet feels like somewhere between midnight and dawn. Passengers scurry onto the platform. There is no conversation, no contact—only a sense of hurry, of avoidance, of people heavy with secrets sliding past each other in silence. Like Balkan ghosts in the night, they disappear into the grey fog, on their way to Iasi: *the city of dreams and whispers.*

It was not my grandparents but a Romanian poet who had described Iasi in such romantic terms. My grandparents, come to think of it, said precious little about the city.

Grandma spoke of Stefanesti, the village of her early girlhood, with such vivacity, such graphic recall, that the town gained life in my mind's eye. London also had been remembered so well and so often that its presence was palpable in the house where I grew up.

It all makes sense. You never forget those early years and you never forget the years that shape and form you. Stefanesti set the stage for Grandma's childhood, as with most of us, a golden time in her life. In London, my grandparents came of age as young marrieds and parents, proud and prosperous. Their time together in Iasi, however, was scant. They were scarcely there a year as newlyweds when Grandpa's brother Zeidel, a fellow cooper in London for a job, wrote to Grandpa urging him to come see "what is going on here."

So it was that I could just about trace footsteps through the village square in Stefanesti. I could see the small orchestra in the bandstand and young people dancing, my grandmother in the sky blue dress she favored. Considering London, I had a vivid picture of the russet brick row house on Redmans Road, and the long line of shops and open air stalls on Mile End down the way. Yet I had only a sketchy notion of Grandma's house in Iasi, offered in scattered reminiscence: shuttered windows, a brass bed, a back porch, and a notorious haystack in which she and Grandpa "got acquainted."

Iasi was well recalled only in places where they courted: that splendid stretch of the Red Bridge, so feverishly imagined by both me and my mother. And the green and gracious Copou Gardens where Great-Uncle Victor ran a beer garden; where my grandparents and their friends came to see and be seen; where strings of bulbs lit up the night with gaiety; and where wine and beer flowed freely and laughter pealed to the sound of violins and concertinas. But that was it. Not much to go on and all the more curious, given the enduring place that Iasi inhabits in the Romanian mystique.

We are making our way down the dark train platform when I can sense the past looking over my shoulder, breathing out of the walls, peering down from the vaulted ceiling. Eighty-plus years ago, my grandparents stood on this very station with two fair-haired children in hand: Jack, a quiet lad of ten, and spirited eight-year-old Betty. They had come to say goodbye to Great-Grandma Sura, to Haim and Roza, and most probably to Monis and his mystery family. They had come to say goodbye before leaving for America.

But my grandparents were changed people. Their vocal patterns were accented by the trim sounds of British speech, and English was the first language of their children. They wore clothes tailored in England. They brought with them a history of life elsewhere, of adopted, beloved nationhood about to be surrendered. My grandparents were then a relatively young and handsome and successful couple who had literally been burned by fate, scarred by a tragedy that propelled them to seek a new life in yet another nation, in "the New World."

My grandparents have come to say goodbye, all right, but this is no ordinary goodbye. This is goodbye to everything that had earlier made them who they were, and there is a catch. When you set sail for America from Europe in this time and place, it is "goodbye" for good. There are no planes, no bargain travel packages, no global Internet or even transatlantic telephones or cables. There is only a long and arduous journey across the sea to an unknown place. When you set sail for America in 1909, unless you are born to wealth, there is no turning back.

Fate hovers over that farewell visit at the precise moment that my grandfather utters three loaded words to Haim, his old army buddy, now brother-in-law, and most probably to Monis. "Come with us," he had said.

But the Grisarius of Iasi have no interest in leaving, and so they stay on in a country that is thriving in a city that is forever elegant in a land that is still magical, unaware that to stay in Romania in 1909, untarnished, floral, and promising as it is, that to continue to dance in this bejeweled and perfumed Romania is to frolic in a fool's paradise.

• • •

25

THERE ARE ROMANIANS WHO HAVE NEVER BEEN TO IASI ... WHEN THERE SHOULD BE NONE!

-Nicolae Iorga, politician and poet

Romanians spell it Iasi but pronounce it Y'ash. In Roma, language of the Gypsies, it is called Yashi. In Yiddish one says Yus, and antique maps often cite the continental if passé Jassy. By any name, Iasi is a special city, faded yet graceful still when I first saw it, and exquisitely situated.

There is a purity to daylight here. From the terrace of our hotel room, you can see it in buttery sunshine that spills onto the streets below, mellow morning contrast to the ghostly fog of the night before. There is something in the air here, something indefinable. A glow. An aura. It softens those white clay apartment houses. It bounces off rooftops and glitters gold from vantage points atop and within the seven hills of the city.

Yes, in the family of fabled cities built upon seven hills, Iasi might seem a poor sister. She is not nearly as famed as Rome, nowhere as ancient as Jerusalem, or modern as Melbourne, or as cosmopolitan as Istanbul. Yet, even among such aristocrats, Iasi holds her own. Consider her pedigree: once and former capital of Moldavia, first city of the united principalities of Walachia and Moldavia, and first capital of Romania before Bucharest.

Neither centuries of war nor decades of political servitude can prevent Iasi from fulfilling a proud destiny as cultural and academic heartland of the nation. From all over the Eastern world, students flock here to study in great universities. In garrets and studios, artists and writers turn paint and pen to words and pictures. In theaters and coffee houses, actors and poets awaken the soul and arouse the psyche. In gleaming opera houses, voices and music ignite the air and stir the heart. Elegant, exuberant Iasi is the nest from which the Romanian spirit takes flight.

Looking at the sun-washed buildings and gilded hills of this thrice-crowned city, one senses why poets deem Iasi, lively, regal and alluring as she is, not just the *city of dreams and whispers*, but also the *city of many loves*. Like all great loves, Iasi is subject to delusion, a victim of fancy. Upon closer investigation, and as the sun begins to dress for afternoon, those romantic quasi-Mediterranean buildings stand naked to the eye. Stripped of early morning light, these are no longer pastel visions of San Francisco or Lisbon or Naples but blocks of Stalinist apartment houses: heavy, plodding, and devoid of color.

Things change. In 1992, before the Revolution, my cousin Sue went to Romania to adopt two children. "There's not a computer in the country," she said, "and no goods on the shelves." Three years later, the first vehicle we spot in the street is a truck carrying computer supplies.

We do find store shelves stocked but often with what we consider eccentric choices from exotic places. In one market we see bar soap from Tunis next to detergent from Egypt. Kiwis and bananas, an unlikely duo, are the only produce for sale in the store, but the open-air market in the center city bursts with crates of fruits and vegetables direct from the countryside. Stalls ripe with ruby tomatoes, purple plums, and green beans beg to be photographed, and I steady my camera.

Seeing me, a peasant woman lifts a watermelon to her shoulder and strikes a jaunty pose, chin high, eyes bold but friendly, feet firm on the ground. Out of nowhere a curly headed moppet runs in front of her, and hogs the camera.

"Get away, *Tzigane* (Gypsy) she yells. My camera captures the boy an instant before he turns and runs, disappearing behind a pile of wood crates and thick-skinned melons, print dresses and shopping bags.

Iasi is a great walking city, so easy to get around in that you'll never get lost. It's a breezy, beauitful, cafe-happy place with lots to see.

My mother and I walk, we sit in cafes, we take in the passing scene. People are everywhere, strolling, strutting, seeing and being seen, and Mom comments on how well they all appear. For a country mired so long in economic misery, everyone looks better than good. Girls in smart high heels clatter down cobbled streets. Young men in baseball caps scoot by on bikes. Rich Romanian wine sparkles in goblets set on tables at outdoor cafes. Mamaliga is curiously missing.

"Maybe they don't have as much as we do," Mom continues, "maybe they are wearing their one and only dress-up outfit, but they haven't lost their dignity." Even the city's canine population trots around with heads held high. We are amazed at how dogs cross the street in unison, unleashed and without collars, wild dogs traveling in well-behaved packs. A helpful clerk in the hotel explains it all.

"The Soviets brought to us not only Communism, but poverty. People were so poor that they couldn't manage to keep their dogs anymore so they set them loose in the parks, and these dogs are their grandchildren."

• • •

"Hello, it's me." The voice belongs to Vonda Condurache, "our woman in Romania." Dark-haired, trim, and stylish in a sleek suit, she proves to be a generous and charming tour guide.

Vonda takes us for a walk down the city's elegant main boulevard. Soviet domination may have robbed Iasi of its old residential architecture yet neither time nor history has diminished the palatial glory of Blvd. Stefan Cel Mare Si S'Fant. Marble opera houses, theaters, libraries, and university buildings overlook manicured lawns and gardens. Shops and stalls showcase modern paintings and crafts, embroidered peasant blouses, and red woven table runners. A horseman carved of black stone stands guard over the Palace of Culture at the head of the street.

All along the avenue, sculpted busts celebrate national artists, from the oft-quoted Mihai Eminescu, regarded by many as the most famous and influential of Romanian poets to Avram Goldfaden, who founded, in Iasi in 1876, what is considered the first professional Yiddish-language theater troupe. Every year The Avram Goldfaden Festival is held here in his honor, and Yiddish theater still flourishes in Iasi with actors who do not speak Yiddish.

Everywhere you can see how Iasi sustains its legacy as cradle of creativity. Cafes and shops line graceful yet vivacious avenues. Art exhibits pop up at every other corner. Students and sculptors and passersby jostle each other. The city has always been this vibrant I am told; yet my grandparents described none of this. Grandpa was a craftsman. Grandma was poorly educated. They came from a different place in society. But they lived right near the heart of the city, right near all this.

Why the silence? Perhaps the joys of Iasi lay buried too far in the past; perhaps my grandparents' time here was overshadowed by life in more dynamic London, and in New York where they would spend the larger part of their lives. Perhaps, like many immigrants, they simply dropped a curtain over the past; perhaps it was too painful to recall that which had been left behind and could never be revisited.

My grandmother did remember the house on Strada Harabuela. I pictured my mother and myself coming upon it, doorway still draped in vines, windows shuttered from the sun, lilacs in bloom. My grandmother's house we would never find. Most of old Iasi has gone down in dust, part of the dictator Ceausescu's plan to make Communism the state culture. In Bucharest, we were told, at the wave of his hand, 19th century villas, grand mansions, and great cathedrals crumbled.

Iasi fared better than Bucharest, largely because of its sizeable college population, it is thought. Fearing student unrest, the mad dictator at least left the city's great main boulevards intact. Though we did happen upon some quaint old areas, most of residential Iasi gave way to endless Soviet-style apartment houses. "Few private homes have been built since the Communist era," Vonda comments.

Some things I would soon learn are best kept in memory. I couldn't wait to see the Red Bridge, so vividly remembered by my grandparents. But the bridge is not red at all. It is grey. It is neither made of gleaming metal nor burnished bricks but of concrete and metal. It is the most pedestrian of pedestrian bridges. "Why was it ever called 'red'?" I ask, looking at this bridge colored as grey as the skin of a mouse.

"Long ago that place upriver was the palace," says Vonda. She points to a magnificent, ornate Palace of Culture, now a military museum. "Upriver," she repeats. Then she utters a revelatory phrase, three words that will precede and haunt almost every detail of every account that we will hear for the rest of our trip: *Legend has it.*

"Legend has it," says Vonda, "that when prisoners of the palace were executed, the river beneath the bridge ran red with blood. And that is why it is known as the Red Bridge."

We stand and watch the clear blue waters of the Prut ripple under the grey walkway of the Red Bridge, where once my grandparents walked, where once they stood, young and sure, on the edge of limitless horizons.

• • •

26
CHURCH

We wander now through the neighborhood of the Red Bridge. Ancient monasteries and churches haunt the hills above. Scoured by time, inspiring and mysterious, these houses of God look down upon the streets where once my grandmother played, strolled, and dreamed: a girl in braids, just moved to the city; a spunky maiden not to be sold short, a new bride, and a young mother. I try to picture her, many years ago, looking up at these very same buildings, even then moored in the past. Did she stare in awe, as we do now? Was she struck by a sense of enigma and miracle? Or did young Clara rush by pulling a shawl around her, a shield of wool against the foreign, medieval secrets of Romanian Orthodoxy?

My grandparents never mentioned these places, significant and romantic as they are. Perhaps because the monastery on the hill was merely a fact of life, seen daily, and taken for granted. Perhaps it came to hide, somewhere in the recesses of memory, forgotten with the passage of time and event.

I want to explore those churches. I want to know what the interior of a Romanian Orthodox Church looks like. I do know that a long time ago in this nation's history, when these religious buildings first rose on that hill, there existed a profound dialogue between the Romanian Orthodox Church and Jewish mystics.

In early evening, we drive with Vonda to a cloister at the summit of the hill overlooking the Red Bridge Quarter. A winding path leads to a small cone-shaped building that could pass for a fairy-tale castle were it not for the cross that tops its turret. A priest stands in front of the wind-battered door, his back to us. Dressed in black vestment and squat hat he does not seem to hear us, Vonda approaches the priest, and he turns. In his hand, he holds a large key as ancient and weather-beaten as the monastery itself. Vonda speaks with him, and then returns to us, smiling. "Father John is just locking up," she says, "but he is pleased that we have come to visit, and he would love to give us a tour."

With his long, full white beard, Father John has the look of a man of great wisdom. As he bows to acknowledge us, rays of kindness warm his ice blue eyes. Possessed of remarkable calm, he turns slowly back to the door, and once again places the great key into the lock. A squeak and a turn, and the door opens. With a sweep of his sleeved hand, Father John gestures for us to enter.

We are in a chapel sweet with the smell of incense and dark with the mystery of the past. Faces of obscure saints, etched in icons of silver and gold, look down from where they live on black velvet walls bathing us with expressions of mercy.

Lanterns and shards of colored glass dangle at varying heights from the ceiling. Carved wooden chairs, thrones of a sort, stare at us throughout the room. Father John begins to speak. In a rich, deep voice resonant with emotion, he offers a precise history of the church from its beginnings in the 16th century to the present.

Vonda translates. "Father tells us how the Romanian Orthodox Church has survived centuries of war and hardship," she explains. "He pleads for peace and forgiveness and worldwide tolerance." Father John's vocal pattern becomes even more heated in a passionate discourse on the endurance of religion in the face of centuries of calamity. Throughout, his fervor never wavers and his gaze remains centered on my mother. She looks away for a moment, eyes cast furtively on the stone floor, then back at the priest. It is a look at once playful and attentive. Mother is one step short of batting her eyes.

Then a breath, and the priest looks at her as if he were searching her soul. "What religion are you?" he asks. Father reels off a series of choices ranging from Romanian Orthodoxy to Roman Catholicism to a host of obscure denominations. Judaism is conspicuously absent. At last, Vonda breaks the news. We are *Evraisca* (Hebrew). With admirable grace, the good priest switches gears.

"Ah," he says, blue eyes still fixed on Mom. "You have a feast this week." The priest flashes a smile at her. "Rosh Hashanah," he goes on, "the feast of the New Year." Mother smiles back at him. I am invisible.

Father John strokes his beard, seemingly lost in thought. He begins to tell us about World War II and he recalls how it was just before Romania entered the War. Fear governed life, and the situation for the nation's Jews had become increasingly grim. Father John was in the army then, and he describes himself as looking rather good in his uniform. He is proud to say that he helped a young Jewish woman escape to Russia by posing as her fiancée. They were planning to be married, he had told the authorities, and she had to get to Russia to visit her family to finalize plans for their wedding.

Father's status as a soldier carried some weight. Kissing his make-believe sweetheart at the border, he watched her cross over into the Soviet Union ... and safety. My mother and I are entranced, but there is something else on the valiant Father's mind. He continues to look at Mom with wonderment. Regaining his voice, he finishes the story with a flourish and takes my mother's hands in his. "I'm 79," he says. "How old are you?"

I wonder at that moment, does Father John see in my mother the Jewish woman whose life he saved a half-a-century ago; does he wonder if, by some miraculous twist of fate and time, she has returned, divine proof of the virtue of goodness. Or has that woman from an earlier time occupied a niche in his heart, like the person you see in passing trains, in the car in the other lane, or just across the street? The man or the woman you never meet, or meet too briefly, and whom you never forget.

I do not remember if my mother actually divulged her age or not but it seems that on this trip, on this journey in and out of the past, in search of lost moments, and here in this ancient place, time stands still.

It is getting late, and Vonda approaches Father John to thank him. She tells him the purpose of our trip. The priest is visibly moved.

Dusk filters through the small windows of leaded glass, and the tawny glow of afternoon turns purple; the same secretive pale shade that fell upon the train station the night we arrived in Iasi. Father John places one arm around my mother's shoulder, and his other arm around me. In the warmth of that sweet-smelling chapel, cloaked in the surpassing light of Romanian twilight, this kind and generous priest gathers us to him.

"What you are doing is very important," he says. "Never forget where you came from. Never forget Romania."

• • •

27
SYNAGOGUE

Vonda Condurache is more than just a native of the city; she is a reporter for
TV-Iasi, and a local celebrity. She is also one of the few young Jews left here,
and an invaluable connection to the Jewish community.

We arrive at the Great Synagogue on Rosh Hashanah, the Jewish New Year that
Father John had spoken of. I fully expect to find records of my great-grandmother's
gravesite here, or at least of her death. If I am lucky, I will find Haim and Roza too.
And if I am really lucky, Monis and the mysterious others.

There was once in Iasi a great Jewish presence. At the outbreak of World War II, about 150,000 people lived here, one-quarter of whom were Jews. Today only several hundred Jews remain, mostly the elderly or those who have been left behind.

Of the approximate 127 synagogues that lined the avenues of the city prior to World War II, only the Great Synagogue survives. It is also the oldest, "built in 1570," a sign on the stucco façade advises, and then "rebuilt in 1670 after an earthquake." Contrary to its imposing name the Great Synagogue is simple in scale and inviting in presence. On its silvery domed roof A Star of David shimmers, like a glimmer in God's eye.

In front of the curled wrought iron gate, a few men and women mill about, and we are shortly showered with greetings. "They knew you were coming," says Vonda. "They were waiting."

Once again we are accidental celebrities. Luisa asks my mother to deliver a message to her cousin in Queens. Radu tells us his son has opened a computer supply store. Miriam says her biggest regret is not moving to Israel with her children. Fate is odd, she goes on, and now her son is leaving Israel for a job in Germany, a plum career move.

We are certain my mother's fluency in Yiddish will come in handy. "You speak Yiddish?" says Titi, a stocky middle-aged woman in a pastel green suit. "Oh my God," she burbles on, switching from Romanian to Yiddish. "No one under sixty speaks Yiddish. Oh my God." A pregnant pause. "Do you speak French?"

"Yiddish? It disappeared," says old Malvina. "Young people, they got *famisht mit de goyim*," literally "mixed up with the non-Jews," undoubtedly the most colorful euphemism ever coined for assimilation. Malvina thinks for a minute, and then looks deep into my mother's eyes. "You speak French?"

Our experience proves the saying, "Old Romanians never die; they just go to Paris." Romanians are so French-crazy that Bucharest was laid out after the French capital. A newsletter from Rom-Sig even features an article on the absence of Hebraic sounding names among Romanian Jews. Citing a study of Jewish women in 1930s Bucharest, it finds few named Rachel or Rebecca, but more than a few named Claudine and Paulette—a phenomenon due, it says, to "snobbishness and an affection for French."

Paris held a fascination for Grandma, too. She claimed that on her way to England, with baby Jack in her arms, a man on the Parisian train platform made a pass at her. She spoke of it often, and every once in a while she mulled over the fact that "Uncle Mauritz went to Paris." I could get no more information on that one. Years later, riding to my uncle's funeral, I sat in the back seat with Mr. Joseph, a friend of his from the Old Country who had lived in the same neighborhood in Iasi.

"Your uncle was a few years older than me," Mr. Joseph said." I always looked up to him. I remember when he went to Paris with three friends, and they came back wearing straw hats. Oh, it was all the fashion. Straw hats and bow ties, bought in Paris." He sighed. I am blown away picturing my quiet uncle, the most devoted husband and father on Earth, a dashing bachelor on the loose in Paris in the 1900s.

The French connection is even more apparent once we enter the synagogue. Grand chandeliers and sophisticated décor sparkle in ornate defiance of the temple's simple exterior. Cases of polished wood and glass showcase antique and fine-looking plates, menorahs, candlesticks, and prayer books.

It gets even more French inside the area of worship. Most of the men in the room are wearing berets instead of the traditional yarmulke, a fashion quirk that makes my style-conscious mother smile broadly.

What the women wear defies category, everything from kerchief and chintzy housedress to stylish frock and new coif. A Romanian-speaking rabbi has been imported from Israel for the holiday. Oblivious to his presence, the women of the Great Synagogue gossip and cackle and snort nonstop throughout the service. You would think they were in a market square rather than a house of worship.

All this drives the rabbi to the end of his spiritual rope. Bypassing the Holy Ark with ungodly speed, he dashes about from one side of the altar to the other, till he dead-ends into a wooden railing, facing the women who yatter on. Wiping his foggy glasses with a rumpled handkerchief, the rabbi rolls his portly frame over the railing, half-weeping and wailing in a shrill voice: "Silencio, mesdames, silencio!"

After the service people swarm around us once again, and everybody has something to say. Titi suggests we visit the Botanica Gradina, part of the Copou Park, which figures fondly in our family's past. Alma tells us she is sure she is related to us. She can see it in our eyes, she says, and to prove the point, she pulls out a photo of her grandson in Israel who bears no resemblance to anyone.

But the best of the bunch is Dr. Cara. A popular lecturer and senior academic, the elderly but spry Cara tells me he is writing a book on the overlooked role of Jews in Romanian arts and letters in the early part the 20th century.

"Most of Romania's great writers and artists were Jews but they often changed their names to hide their Jewish identities." He mentions Tristan Tsara and Marcel Yanku as examples. "So we have not gotten the credit we deserve for our very big contributions." We talk and talk and before saying goodbye, I comment on the professor's surname: Cara. "It is such a beautiful sounding name," I say.

"It's not my real name. What you might call a professional name."

"What is your real name?"

"Schwartz."

• • •

Later on we meet with the Jewish Community Organization. Mr. Pinscu, who is president, remembers a few Grisarius he knew personally but no one he mentions rings a bell. Getting down to business, Mr. Pinscu opens an ancient roll book, and he pores through page after musty page of the dead and buried Jews of Iasi. All the faded ink on all the withered paper yields no mention of Sura, Haim, or Roza Grisariu, no less Monis and his family. I remember the stories about that final letter from Romania to my grandmother, saying that her mother had died. "Well, the others might have moved elsewhere," I say, "but I am certain my great-grandmother died here."

Mr. Pinscu, the community members and Vonda, my mother, and I put our heads together and we all reach the same conclusion. Most probably Great-Grandma Sura's body was moved to Stefanesti, to be buried alongside her husband. There is a Jewish custom I rather like, that of placing a stone on a gravesite you've visited to show you were there, proof of tribute. What an honor, I thought, what a wonderful gesture, for Mom and me to take a stone, a pebble, a shard lifted from the soil of Stefanesti, and place it upon the forgotten gravestones of my great-grandparents.

We search more records. Neither Haim nor Roza nor Monis and his phantom family have been buried in Iasi either. Our chances of finding information on any of their whereabouts or of meeting someone who knew the family are pretty slim, given how long ago they lived, the upheaval that shook the land during World War II, the Holocaust, and the fear and suspicion that plagued postwar Romania.

Most of Romania's Jews, we are told, moved to Israel under Ceausescu, in the 1960s, not because of anti-Semitism but because Romania was in a shambles. Reckless and ill-conceived fiscal policies brought the nation to economic ruin, while a maniacally brutal Red regime spawned a culture of fear, a world defined by sudden arrest, and disappearance.

For Jews, Israel offered a portal to liberty and a better life. In the 1960s, the Free World applauded Ceausescu as the only Communist leader of the day to maintain friendly ties with the Jewish State. In reality, he was fattening his wallet by selling Jews to Israel, so many shekels per head.

• • •

We stand in the Jewish cemetery at Iasi. Framed by a scenic bluff, rows and rows and rows of pale curved gravestones line up in stately symmetry, a single Star of David etched into the middle of each gently turned arch. Overlooking all, a simple stone memorial pays profound homage to victims of an infamous massacre during the Holocaust. "If your relatives weren't caught up in that," we are told, "they may be around…somewhere."

I know little about Romania during the war. I have come upon references to the pogrom in Iasi in books on the Holocaust. Occasional, grim photos show streets littered with bodies, and tracks lined with dusty and menacing wagon cars. Captions are few, details sparse. "Ah," says Vonda, in response to my asking what happened. "Here come the stories."

She tells us that in the 1930s government restrictions against Romania's Jews grew in number and severity. Within a few years, the world would close in on the Jews of Iasi specifically, and the reigning Fascist regime ordered Jewish men of all ages to show up at the big courtyard of the police station. Those that appeared were carted off to God-knows-where. Most weren't heard from again.

Fearful to live through, to be sure, especially if it was your son or father or nephew, but not nearly as gruesome as what befell Jews elsewhere in Europe. Why, I wonder, are there no records for our relatives: had my uncles and boy cousins vanished, too, into that dark and bitter Romanian night?

• • •

28
BOTOSANI

We are on our way to Stefanesti, about an hour north of Iasi, to see Grandma's village, and to search for the gravestones of her parents. White-capped mountains and lime green fields seed the Moldavian landscape with notions of Switzerland. Except for a passing peasant woman in a dark print dress and kerchief, there is not a soul in sight. Fetchingly shy, the peasant woman waves at us even as she looks to the ground, murmuring *buna dimineaza* (good day).

Seamlessly those white towers recede into the sky above and the road below turns into a long, lone strip of grey pebbles and brown dust. We bump and bounce along until halted by a parade of blank-faced women. Dressed in black they emerge from nowhere. In their arms, they carry long loaves of braided breads with twisted tips pointing upward. A string of somber men in dark suits trail behind, lost in their own private worlds. We wait for the mourners to pass.

Other than that strange funeral march our trip is distinguished by fields of cease-lessly green grass, crystal skies, and cracked dinnerware at a restaurant where we stop for lunch. "The Revolution couldn't afford new dishes," quips our driver. Again mamaliga is not on the menu.

I wonder about Stefanesti. There are no Jews in the village today. Those who remain in the area live in nearby Botosani, a larger town and county seat. Vonda has arranged for us to meet the head of the Jewish community in Botosani, but we cannot find the place. Jumping out of the car in the center of town, Vonda stops the first person she sees, a freckle-faced young woman with short red hair. After a surprisingly long chat, Vonda comes back wearing a big smile. "That was Mrs. Cohen," she says. Winking, she adds, "Mrs. Cohen can tell us how to get to the Jewish Community Center."

On the main street of Botosani, where Jews are nearly fiction, we have found Mrs. Cohen. Yet despite Mrs. Cohen's directions, we still cannot find our way. For fifty frustrating minutes, we drive through the colorless streets of this terminally grey city and, then stumble upon the Jewish Community Center.

Outside the building is seedy yet dignified; inside it is no different. Lace curtains cover the wooden frames of long windows. A quality of sepia, of neglected Old World charm, pervades the room, from the faded tan walls to the warm wood of a walnut desk and armoire, sole pieces of furniture. Spartan and antique, the room pays mute testimony to the lost world of Jewish life in Moldavia, an area once called "a greenhouse of Jewry."

We are introduced to the head of the Jewish Community Center, an impeccable little man; white hair parted and slicked down, grey suit and tie pressed and neat. He begins to speak in Romanian, but when my mother asks if he speaks Yiddish, his face lights up. In a chivalrous bow to the past, his bespectacled eyes focus solely on Mom, and he begins to speak, softly...

I listen carefully. This is not the Yiddish that I am accustomed to. No "oy oy oy's," no Borscht Belt jokes, no rising inflections, or self-belittling humor, no gut wrenching, breast-beating histrionics.

Rather his speech pattern is gracious, his vocabulary flowery, his delivery steeped in the niceties of a bygone time.

"It does my heart great pleasure to welcome you," the man says in tones as genteel and tired as the décor of this room.

"What a beautiful country," my mother offers.

"Yes, but the life here is hard," comes the reply. "Very hard."

The director calls into the room a courtly gent in his seventies who has been chosen or volunteered to be our guide in Grandma's village.

Mr. Seygall, a violinist with the Botosani Philharmonic, grew up in Stefanesti some time after my grandmother lived there. Dressed in bow tie and jacket, he bows deeply and begins to speak, his voice as silvery as his tousled hair.

Given Mr. Seygall's generation, the rest of the conversation is conducted completely in Romanian, with Vonda translating. He was a boy in Stefanesti about two to three decades after Grandma's time, he says. With a gentlemanly bow, the violinist casts a glance at my mother, a proper peek that lingers a moment too long. She stares back. Once again, as in the monastery, I am rendered all but unseen.

"It will be my pleasure to be your guide to the town where your mother and I were both born," he says to Mom. He smiles a little more broadly, bows once again, and kisses her on both cheeks.

• • •

29
STEFANESTI

We ride in silence, Vonda, Mr. Seygall, my mother, and I. Mom points to passing signposts. Stefanesti is not far off.

S-te-fa-nes-ti.

I can hear the word, just as it was spoken in my youth.

Shh te fah ne sssht...

Listen to the sound of it. That mysterious *ssshhh*, as if the speaker were keeping a secret, finger placed to lips in warning. Hear it in the *sssshhs* that haunt Romanian words and place names.

Bucuresti. Ploesti. Pitesti.

Listen to that same seductive *sssshhh*, as it builds to a crescendo, cresting into the unheard "ti" … of a sudden evaporating into the air, falling off the face of the Earth.

Shhh-te-fa-ne-ssshhh- t'

"What does it mean?" I say out loud.

Vonda looks at me, curious.

"Stefanesti," I repeat, a name so familiar, yet without definition. "What does it mean? How did the town get its name?"

A smile plays on Vonda's lips, a story brewing in her coffee brown eyes. Mr. Seygall, quiet till now, breaks out in a shy, knowing grin. A moment pause, and then the tale unfolds in classic Romanian fashion. …

"Legend has it," Vonda begins, "that a long time ago, centuries ago, when the town was young, even smaller than it is today and called by another name, that in those early days a young man galloped into the center of the village, out of nowhere, in a state of great excitement."

My mother and I listen, transported through the years, the rest of the world disappearing even as tidy pastel houses of the village appear in the distance.

"This young man," Vonda goes on, "swore that he had just seen a band of guardsmen escorting a great nobleman on a white steed, and that this great nobleman is none other than Stefan cel Mare (Stephen the Great), Prince of Moldavia, protector of the kingdom who had fought off the Ottomans, the Poles, and the Hungarians, all of whom sought to conquer the land. This young man had recognized the valiant one from his likeness on a coin."

"And?" I interrupt.

"And," she says, "they all went wild. Just think, a figure of such enormous importance riding into this little out-of-the-way place. What to do? At once, the leaders of the town summoned the most prosperous and esteemed citizens for a secret meeting, and when it was over, the wealthy and the wise mounted their horses and rode slowly to the village line.

"There they waited and waited, until, on the horizon, came a band of warriors on chestnut horses. In the middle of these guardsmen, rode the remarkable nobleman, taller than the treetops and supreme in bearing on a horse as white as fallen snow.

"Approaching the nobleman, hats in their hands, the wealthy and the wise bowed, possessed of awe as they were, and even fear. Then, with great respect, the mayor stepped forward and dared address the nobleman directly.

"Tell us, honored one, is it true? Are you Stefan?"

"Stefanesti! (*I am Stephen!*)"

"And that," says Vonda, "is how the town got its name".

Modest solid homes of pale clay with high windows rise behind wooden fences in Stefanesti, just as they did in my grandmother's day. She remembered her house on Strada Noroba Guiler, and I wanted to find it. "No," Vonda cautions, "We cannot explore these streets. This is a Gypsy town."

Gypsies! Why not visit the Gypsies? I stand and stare at windows sealed by wooden shutters, wondering what strange dangers or what exotic world lurk within? Are the Gypsy women as beautiful as Grandma said? Did colored beads sparkle still in their black braids? Were the men mustachioed, with dark eyes that held secrets? Was there an ancient woman in the corner who practiced Gypsy magic? Did copper pots and pitchers gleam on shelves within those houses, set out for repair? I stare and stare at those wooden shutters, wondering. Everyone else heads off, but I stay behind. Alone, on that cobbled road, I wait for Gypsy fiddles to play.

• • •

Mr. Seygall proudly points out the primary school of Stefanesti. My grandmother was a girl in braids when it was built, as far back as 1885 or so, and she still spoke about it with wonder some seventy years later and a continent away.

That primary school became a turning point in Grandma's life—but for the wrong reason. In her day, as now, such a school was cause for pride in so small a town. My grandmother said, and this never ceases to surprise me, that education was compulsory in this area of Romania in her time, and the authorities went door to door to make sure that all children were attending school. I later thought how emblematic this was of Romania then, entering the modern world at a time when the country was prosperous and its promise seemingly limitless.

Great-Grandpa Hirsicu saw to it that his sons went to school. They had to read and write to make their way in this new and modern world. But Great-Grandma Sura would have none of it where little Clara was concerned. Pious and provincial, she saw public school as suspect, a passage to increased intimacy with the world at large.

Sura Grisariu was certain that if her only daughter went to this primary school, chances of her running off with a non-Jew would increase tenfold. I believe she was right. Public school clinched the process of nationalization. Once you met and mingled with "the others," you became more Romanian and less Jewish. So, when the authorities came to call, Grandma's mother hid her in the hayloft, paving the course of her future life under a pile of straw.

Innately clever and possessed of keen wit, my grandmother would forever be envious and enamored of neighbor girls and cousins who went on to the *gymnazia*; who could read the works of Balzac and Goethe in the original French and German; who could recite the poetry of Mihai Eminescu by heart; or read the local papers and write letters in Romanian, in fancy cursive script that drew praise from teachers and parents, and suitors.

In a world that was rapidly changing, my grandmother was left behind. It was a loss she would lament to her dying day.

We sit on park benches watching Gypsy boys kick a soccer ball around in the town square, making dust rise and fall upon patches of dry grass. A soft breeze stirs the air. Leaves come tumbling down from ancient trees.

Mr. Seygall points to an abandoned platform where once, he tells us, a bandstand stood. The grass was green and full then, he says. Sketching out the phantom band and spirited dancers, he ends every memory with a worshipful "Eminescu says," ceremonial entrée to a quote from the great Romanian poet.

My grandmother's stories of the boundless dances of her girlhood shimmer in the vivid pools of Mr. Seygall's memories. I try to imagine her, near that bandstand when the paint was fresh. I see her, young and flaxen-haired, flushed and fair, dancing till the moon came out, so she said, in a dress the color of the heavens.

I hear the rustle of long skirts, and the sound of heels crunching brittle leaves. Shoes, high-button shoes with graceful heels, break into departed dances, rousing ghosts of my grandmother's girlhood.

"Eminescu speaks of autumn," Mr. Seygall whispers, in triple homage to the revered poet, to the red and brown leaves that carpet the square, and, I am thinking, to the lost past. Mr. Seygall's voice trails off, and Eminescu's words linger in the crisp air.

Now it's autumn, leaves roam and scatter.
And you're reading old letters, tattered and fading.
And retrace a whole lifetime in just one hour.

• • •

There are no Jews in Stefanesti today. Hardly any have been buried in the Jewish cemetery here since the 1960s. Tumbledown tombstones, covered in wild vines and weeds, lie about helter skelter, like a Balkan version of the cemetery in *Great Expectations*. Inscriptions hint at tales of lost lives. Tania, died in a bombardment. David, moved to Bucharest, buried here in his hometown. Darling Papa. Beloved Mother.

A gatekeeper, hired by the Jewish community in Botosani, wipes sweat off the bandana tied round her forehead, then smears her hands on her apron. She is fidgety and flighty, squawking this and that in a high-pitched voice, but friendly. Her cow, tied to ramshackle fencing, lets out a mournful moo or two. Geese scurry between gravestones, a surreal footnote to dead ancestors and fading history.

Eager to be of help, the gatekeeper leads us on a winding path through dirt, weed, and stone, but the graves of Hirsicu and Sura Grisariu are nowhere. I am bewildered. There were several thousand Jews who lived here once, but barely a few hundred tombstones.

Later on, I am told that it is the custom in this part of the world to remove old tombstones and use them for building; and with the passage of the years graves are dug on top of each other. Then again, the German Army marched through this area on their way to Russia. Who knows how many fierce boots trampled the earth, or what damage they did. Who knows how many dead rest above the bed of dirt where my great-grandparents slumber.

Disappointment weighs heavily on me. I thought it a long shot and unlikely that we would find clues to the fate of Monis and even Haim and Roza, not to mention Monis's wife and especially his children. But I tell Mr. Seygall that we had hoped at the very least to find my great-grandparents, to place stones of remembrance upon their gravesites.

Mr. Seygall looks at me in surprise. "We do not do that here," he says, explaining that the local custom is to light a candle. I wonder how and where the custom of placing a stone upon a grave originated. I have heard conflicting explanations of its origin at different funerals conducted by different rabbis. Perhaps it is not religious in origin at all.

We enter an abandoned area, ringed by rusted fencing that has become unhinged by time and lies low to the ground. We stand, a long way from home, my mother and I, lighting candles in tribute to sadly, shockingly missing ancestors. Mr. Seygall nods kindly at me. Once again he kisses my mother on both cheeks.

"It does not matter that you did not find them," he says. "What matters is that you came."

• • •

30
OUR LAST NIGHT

Stylish women in broad-brimmed hats sashay down a tree lined boulevard in Iasi. Devilishly handsome young couples, looking like they stepped out of café society, raise champagne glasses in an apparent toast to good times ahead. Nothing could be further from the truth.

We are gathered around a long wooden dining room table in the cheery apartment of Vonda's mother, looking at old family photos. Radiating a sense of chic and high spirits, these photos might have been snapped in prewar Paris. But this is prewar Iasi, and these are Romanian Jews, making merry in a glitzy world that is about to darken and disown them with a vengeance.

How could these people, Romanian Jews, be sitting pretty in a place already inflamed by anti-Semitism, a country simmering in the heat of a hateful fever burning its way through Europe with all the fury of a fiery Holocaust. As if reading my mind, Vonda's mother says: "These were taken just before the lights went out."

"You mean when they summoned the men to the police station?" I asked.

She shrugs, and then bustles off to the kitchen where Vonda's husband Daniel is busy preparing a "surprise" for us.

This is our last night in Iasi. Tomorrow we are off by train for a visit in Bucharest, before flying back home. We had wanted to take Vonda and her husband out for dinner, but they kept putting us off.

Meeting Vonda in front of our hotel, she confesses that they have planned a something special for us at her mother's.

Earlier in the day, just before dinnertime, when we were waiting for Daniel, whom we'd not yet met, I was struck by the passing parade of spiffy looking young people. I had to remind myself: this is a city packed with college students. A young woman catches my eye. Sauntering past in scanty shorts and halter-top, she holds a fluffy white ball of a poodle in her arms, curly white fur offset by a rhinestone collar. "After the war people couldn't afford to keep their dogs, so they let them loose in the park," Vonda had told us. Comes the Revolution, I thought. No economic assessment more revealing than a young woman nuzzling a pampered pooch when once city parks were alive with abandoned pets.

To complete the picture, a snappy little sports car zooms to a halt in front of us and out comes Daniel. Sweet-faced, fortyish, and sandy haired, he bows deeply, a gallant old-world dip that honors my mother's presence. Then, much to her delight, he kisses her hand. "Very Romanian!" says Vonda.

We climb into Daniel's little car and take off, weaving through the streets of Iasi as dusk begins to work its purple magic over the city. Getting out of the car in front of one of those Soviet-style apartment houses we have seen only from a distance, I am aware of how dark it is now, and I mean *dark*. The barely lit street is beyond dim and the apartment house is no better.

Entering the vestibule plunges us into a universe devoid of light. We walk softly, clutching at air till a banister makes its presence felt. Prisoners of perpetual night, we feel our way onto the silhouette of an unseen stairway. Daniel flicks on a cigarette lighter, and we join hands to make our way up the stairway, step by step in secure unison, blessed by a little flame.

A knock on the door is answered by a sweet voice, a musical voice, a woman's voice. The door swings open and warm light from within floods the hall. A middle-aged woman with dark reddish brown hair stands in the doorway, graceful and airy in a mauve dress of organdy. Vonda's mother is thrilled to have foreigners visit, but flustered at such short notice. Her apartment is pleasant, modest, and sensibly furnished. A large breakfront dominates the room, its honey colored, inlaid wood polished to a gleaming sheen.

On my second trip to Romania, twelve years later, I would visit more than one apartment and find variations of the same living room centerpiece: a shining display case for all the comforts of family life, from bric-a-brac salvaged through war and hard times to stemware and stoneware heralding better days. Two thick pink ceramic candlesticks flank the center shelf of a handsome cabinet. "They look almost religious," my mother whispers.

This, as it turns out, is no ordinary dinner, but a theme banquet of foods that would have been served and savored in my grandmother's day. Dinner proceeds and the table is set with the obligatory eggplant, smoked and oiled, spiced and mashed. Soft white cheese akin to cottage cheese shares a plate with sweet green peas, no sheep cheese, though it is mentioned, and no end of red Romanian wine.

Now Daniel summons Vonda into the kitchen. We hear clattering and subdued laughter. Sly glances are exchanged at the table, and then Vonda emerges, platter in hand.

"Mamaliga!" she announces.

"And what a mamaliga," my mother says, and she is right. This is a giant puff of cornmeal the likes of which I have never seen before, a mountain of gold so feathery and generous that it threatens to take off and take over the room.

Daniel tells us that his mother sent the cornmeal from her village, not far away. He also explains that the fluffy mountain of mamaliga was traditionally cooked in a big cast iron pot called a *caeun*. Its heavy bottom molded the mamaliga to perfection while an ironclad lining kept the cornmeal warm. From time immemorial and through my grandmother's day, he says, every family in Romania cooked mamaliga in a *caeun*. Each family also had its own wooden ladle, individually engraved, for stirring the mamaliga while it spat into the air and thickened in the pot.

It took a while, but eventually I understood why when I was growing up, Grandma just wouldn't make mamaliga. It wasn't a question of cornmeal, yellow or white, stone ground or not, Romanian or American. It was the absence of ritual and comfort. No family ladle. No big black *caeun*. No mamaliga.

It wasn't the same.

• • •

31
RAILS

*D*ue *billete din Bucuresti,* I say to the woman behind the ticket booth, in Romanian and with great authority.

"Two tickets to Bucharest," the ticket lady answers in perfect English. Even after a month here, and despite constant applause for my flawless Romanian enunciation, I am still visibly American.

Unlike our previous cross-country ride, this train to Bucharest is first-rate and up-to-date. No prehistoric mud-spattered exterior, no torn and tattered interior. No, sir, this choo-choo is as streamlined and shiny as a spaceship.

A middle-aged man, bald and bespectacled, collars me in the corridor. "Is this going to Bucharest?" he asks, in English, mind you.

"Yes," I answer, and he tells us that he is an Israeli, originally from Iasi. The train, we will find out, is crawling with Israelis of Romanian origin. Some come back to pay gravesite visits, others just for nostalgia.

One of our compartment mates turns out to be a young Israeli woman, born in Romania. The other is a peasant woman with two children.

Physically and temperamentally they are at opposite ends of the spectrum. No makeup for the peasant lady whose pure profile and demeanor are wondrously maternal, a sensibility enhanced by the constant attention she lavishes on two darling children. She does not speak English, and we never find out her name.

Much makeup for the Israeli woman. A glamorous Middle-Eastern beauty she is, with chiseled features, grey eyes framed by dark charcoal and smoky eye shadow, and lips outlined in Technicolor red. Vastly different though they are, these two strike up an unlikely bond: the Israeli singing to the children in Romanian while the peasant mother fascinated by her new and fashionable friend.

We never know the Israeli woman's name either. But there is an allure about her, such a sense of intrigue, that she might well have been called Mata Hari. It gets better. She tells us she is married to an Egyptian, and is fluent in Arabic and English as well as Hebrew and Romanian. The couple has two children who, in their parents' absence, shuttle back and forth between Cairo and Tel Aviv, spending alternate weeks with both sets of grandparents.

My mother just eats all of this up, and when we are left alone for a moment, she assesses the situation, as only she can: "Her husband must be very good looking," she concludes, as if sexy good looks could be the only thing that could ever bring about a successful Arab-Israeli union.

We are barely out of Iasi when the train chugs to a stop at a small city. It seems like a place of no consequence, so it's a while before I notice the signpost. "Oh, my God!" I say, pointing the name of the town out to my mother.

VASLUI

So, this is where the Vasluieur Fraternal Association got its name. Our retreat from Vaslui is slow at first, but once this sleek, stainless steel bullet of a train gains speed, it zooms through the countryside. Even service on board is refreshingly streamlined, no little juice men, no mountain of tickets. This, I am thinking, is modern Romania, riding the rails into a bright new future.

Suddenly the train screeches to a halt, throwing us all out of our seats. Suitcases and shopping bags tumble off shelves, compartment doors fly open, passengers shriek, and sounds of pandemonium bounce up and down the length of the train. An ungodly scream rises from the side of the tracks, piercing every corridor and cubicle on board: the voice of a man, rippled with sorrow and broken by grief.

We rattle to a sudden standstill in a small village in God Knows Where. It is early morning. Some folk peer out of cottage windows, others pour out of their doors. Some women are still in nightgowns, others in peasant skirts and kerchiefs. Young men appear in shirtsleeves and shorts, others in overalls. All wear expressions of shock and dismay, concern and suspicion.

Passengers buzz around the train windows like bees to honey. No one knows what has happened and everyone wants answers. As morning turns to noon, whispers rise into a thundering crescendo, a chorus of welcome: the transportation police have arrived. Uniformed officers shout at our conductor and he shouts back. Hands fly. Tempers flare. More than one passenger feels compelled to offer an opinion. More hands fly. The first act of the opera is in full force.

We wait. We wonder. Word spreads from car to streamlined car. This lightning streak of a train, all chrome and steel, whizzing along at supersonic speed, modern as they come, has just run over a horse. His master, bereft beyond words, falls to his knees and beseeches the heavens.

Weeping uncontrollably, the poor man is removed from the scene, a uniformed officer at each arm, helping him along. My mother and I, along with the Israeli beauty, the peasant woman, and her children return to our compartment. Our fellow passengers retreat to their cars. Sadness falls upon the train. Out of nowhere, the bald and bespectacled middle-aged Israeli man pops his head in our door. Compelled to commentary, he clears his throat. "No doubt about it," he says, "that poor fellow lost more than his livelihood." The Israeli thinks for a minute. "When that man lost his horse, he lost his best friend!"

The peasant woman nods in agreement, although it is apparent from the glazed look in her kind eyes that she does not understand a word the Israeli man has said.

Mata Hari pays no attention to any of it. She is beside herself. She confides, much to my mother's enjoyment, that she is en route to Paris to meet her husband on a matter cloaked in secrecy. For whatever private, dark reasons, our woman of mystery cannot or will not reveal the nature of her mission but offers one tantalizing clue: a dire exchange of money is involved.

Trackside, tempers flare and voices rise. Act Two of the ongoing opera is gaining steam and a dramatic duet between transportation police and rail authorities is hitting notes that could shatter glass. Neither time nor money nor passion nor need can deny the Romanian penchant for high drama or the willingness to waste time.

Our blazing bullet of a train, refreshingly modern and blindingly shiny, arrives in Bucharest six hours late.

• • •

32
BUCHAREST

"According to Romanian legend," so the guidebook says, "the city of Bucharest was founded on the banks of the Dambovita River by a shepherd named Bucur, whose name means "joy." Bucur's flute playing reputedly dazzled all who heard it, and his hearty wine from nearby vineyards so endeared him to the local traders, that they gave his name—"joy"—to the new city.

You wouldn't know it from the train station, a cavernous space framed by erector-set lattices above, heavy iron gates without, and hustle bustle within, which is what you'd expect in a central hub of a city numbering two-and-a-half-million. Gritty is the word. More than one person is sacked out on a bench, and a couple of Gypsies huddle near the massive entry gates. Dressed in wildly colorful robes, they give us the onceover as we pass by.

I have been cautioned against spending time in the capital city because "they are westernizing it" and it is overpriced.

There was a time when Bucharest was hailed the most buoyant of Balkan capitals. To the world, she was the "Paris of the East," and to all accounts, it was a title well earned. Bucharest, like its Gallic counterpart, shone as a sophisticated destination defined by fine wine and good food. Here nightlife flourished, style triumphed, and romance blossomed behind shuttered windows, in smoky cafes, and under darkened archways.

Big, cosmopolitan Bucharest was a happening place, an enchanting warmly lit city of cobblestone lanes, old-world villas, and lavish apartments. Came the Jazz Age, and Bucharest became a chic showcase of moderne Bauhaus architecture, its newer neighborhoods defined by glass and light and space.

Dreamy, smart, amorous Bucharest was undone not so much by war but by a ruthless Red dictatorship that turned plenty to naught, radiance to ashes, and confidence to desperation.

Bucharest in 1994 was still big for sure, and busy, but a shadow of its former self. Time and ill fortune had turned it into an architectural hodgepodge of ramshackle yet atmospheric 19th century villas and cold no-frills new housing. Monstrous Soviet public structures offer proof in lime and mortar of Ceausescu's diabolical plan to raze Romania, placing a Communist mask over the nation's peerless cultural and architectural identity.

Raped of elegance and drained of spirit, this Bucharest is a city at a crossroads. Most of its grand mansions live in memory, but there is still enough of the old stuff around, waiting to be spruced up and noticed. Thanks to dictatorial lack of sophistication, much of the city's Bauhaus legacy survives and the government has embarked upon a campaign of education and preservation.

There is in the air a sense of possibility. One sees it in restaurants that aspire to chic, in waiters who still conduct themselves with international flair, and in young people, looking good, who scoot by on bikes or make their way through the streets with a sense of purpose. One also senses it in the abundance of German tourists, enjoying good Romanian wine and food in a city seeking to recapture its lost reputation for happy-go-lucky hospitality. Twelve years later, I would return and find a city being touted by tourist agents as "The Paris of the 21st Century."

Imagining Bucharest, but having no concept of what the near future would hold, my thoughts are interrupted by my mother's voice, uttering one startling word. "Sturgeon!" she says, as if having just given birth.

"Sturgeon?" I ask.

"Sturgeon!" she responds, reliving a food moment, pinnacle of a previous trip to Romania with my stepfather. They had come here on a guided tour in the 1970s during the reign of Ceausescu, when tourism was confined to carefully orchestrated visits to select cities in carefully considered areas.

"We weren't able to get to Iasi, but Mike and I had this terrific dinner in Bucharest. It was in this lovely restaurant on a lake, and we ate fresh grilled sturgeon. I never tasted anything like it."

Thanks to the concierge at our hotel, we know where we are going. A cab drives us along a wide boulevard that is Parisian in spirit, but dusty and rumpled.

Older sections come fleetingly into view, somehow surviving the siege of Ceausescu. Winding, cobbled alleys offer glimpses into faded glory. Rows of rococo buildings huddle together in a wondrously Old World streetscape, an urban geography that inspires exploration. You want to stop the cab, get out, and take an old-fashioned walk.

Hanging shingles advertise goods and services, but shop windows whiz by too quickly to reveal the bottles and boxes on display. I wonder where those winding alleys lead, what gems wait to be discovered behind the well-washed windows of those storefronts, and what secrets simmer within those walls. I know now why the Romanian Jewish journalist and radio commentator, Andres Codrescu, calls Bucharest "the magical city of my youth."

As if summoning the city's former grandeur, and to prove a continental point, we drive past Bucharest's version of a Paris landmark: the city's very own Arc de Triomphe. A short while later we arrive at the restaurant of choice. Mother is right.

With its woodsy and warm décor, this place can hold its own in any major dining capital. Young waiters in quasi-Tyrolean uniforms bow and scrape and take our orders. Stewards pour wine with a master's flourish. Fresh caught sturgeon is brought to the table, on a platter, grilled to perfection, and garnished with curlicue greens. We dine, looking out over the tree-draped still waters of Lake Snagov, a tranquil refuge in the middle of the busy capital.

Contrary to what we had been told, Bucharest deserves more time. A day and a half leaves us not a moment to spare, and we spend the end of our short visit trying to absorb the architectural stew around us. Two buildings capture our imaginations. You couldn't miss the Parliament building, Ceausescu's gigantic dubious monument to pomposity. Currently billed as the second largest building in the world, it looks like it could devour the entire city.

We make a point of seeing the Royal Palace. Pillared to a fare-thee-well and capped in bronze, the Palace gifts a full city block with passé majesty. Here the royal family once feuded and frolicked. Here affairs of the state and of the heart were spawned and spurned, nurtured or overturned. Here Ceausescu held court at overblown Communist ceremonies. Here finally, bullets shot down his mad schemes and brutal reign, carving scars into the Palace walls, permanent souvenirs of the Romanian Revolution.

Even the wounds of uprising cannot lessen the romance of this grand building. But Mother and I have our own special reason for seeing The Palace. We stand there, looking this way and that, trying to catch a glimpse of the secret passageway of the mistress to the king, the woman all Romania and the world at large once whispered about: Magda Lupescu.

• • •

33
ROYAL SCANDAL

Magda and the king. There was a time when their every move set hearts of the world aflutter, when society rags and gossip mags chronicled where they went, what they did, and with whom they hobnobbed. By my time the romance of Magda Lupescu and King Carol barely smoldered in the public memory, but in our house its flame never died.

It is one of Grandpa's favorite stories, and he tells it over and over without ever missing a beat. We have a vested interest in the king's mistress. She is of humble origin, she comes from Iasi, and she is Jewish or reportedly half-Jewish. Born Elena Lupescu, daughter of a junk dealer, she is mistakenly dubbed Magda by a newspaper reporter—and the name sticks.

"Madame Lupescu and the king met at a big dance," Grandpa would begin, setting the stage. Future research reveals that they met at a military ball, and neither was single. She, the willowy, titian-haired wife of an army officer, was what used to be called "a man's woman." He was married to Helen of Greece and proud papa of the eventual King Michael, all of which didn't put the brakes on. Mustachioed and dapper, and a devotee of the high life, Carol was what used to be called a "roué."

"Legend has it," Grandpa would continue, with a delectable grin, "that Carol and Lupescu took one look at each other, danced around the room, and disappeared." Eyewitnesses say the seductive redhead and the flirtatious king twirled around the ballroom, indeed once, maybe twice, and then vanished from sight. Two or three days later, while the world waited and wondered, they resurfaced in a swanky villa on the Riviera, proceeding to live "in sin" with an impudence that was simultaneously condemned and envied.

In Bucharest, the king sets Lupescu up in a villa outside the city. Outraged, Carol's wife calls it quits, and Lupescu becomes the undisputed woman behind the throne. *Vanity Fair* calls her the Romanian DuBarry, a tag that only magnifies her status as an object of glamour and controversy.

The Romanian DuBarry! That stroke of the pen wins Lupescu an honored place alongside not only DuBarry but de Pompadour and Nell Gwynn, right up there with Lola Montez and Lady Castlemaine, not quite blue bloods in the purple halls of the great mistresses of imperial Europe. Yet Madame Lupescu stands apart from the others.

Cosmopolitan dubs her an international siren who rules "behind curtains of gauze," and the effect on the public is enthralling. In an age of waning royalty, Magda Lupescu is a royal favorite—and the world cannot get enough of her and her illicit regal lover. Notoriety becomes them, and it will be their undoing.

This is Europe in the 1930s. Dictatorial madness is epidemic on the continent and Romania has caught the fever. Too soon, the nation's carefree ways will be crushed by the weight of the Iron Guard. No Fascist regime was more aptly named, or more anti-Semitic."And here," Grandpa would say, "is where Lupescu and Carol become a story of great love."

My grandfather is right. The last thing the figurehead king of a country like this Romania needs is a Jewish mistress. Carol could have ditched her. He could have sold her up the river. He could have made her "disappear." Or, at the very least, spirited her off in the dead of night to safety in Russia. Ousted by a coup, he elects none of those options but flees the country with her, with a fortune in art, furs, antiques, and jewelry in tow.

Word spreads quickly throughout Romania that the deposed king and his alluring redhead are on the run, heading west by train. In such a world as this, nothing could be more contemptuous than a fugitive ruler and his Jewish mistress, bound no doubt for a better place, and certainly a life of contraband luxury.

Murder is in the air and on a scheduled stop at westernmost Timisoara assassins besiege the train. Dodging an explosion of shots the couple cheat death by taking shelter in the royal bathtub.

Refugee lovers in a continent gone mad, Magda and the king make it to Portugal. From the port of Lisbon, Carol tries to gain entry to the United States, but his politics are suspect and his pleas for asylum fall on unhearing ears. Cuba likewise says "no."

Marooned on the edge of Europe, bereft of legitimacy or country, Carol and Lupescu are at bay in a world without mercy. With unerring style, the couple become a sparkling fixture in a colony of royal exiles, waiting it out in wartime Lisbon. Eventually the king and his longtime mistress make their way to Brazil, finding safe haven in Rio de Janeiro.

It is 1947, and Lupescu has reached the end of the line. Even her celebrated glamour is no match for cancer. In a deathbed ceremony by candlelight in Rio, King Carol marries his longtime mistress, making her officially the Princess Elena of Romania.

"By some miracle of God," Grandpa would say, "Madame Lupescu rallies, and she goes on to outlive King Carol by many more years." Then there follows a long dramatic pause while we all sit silent pondering the whims of fate and the power of love, and then Grandpa would raise a finger, pointing upward, as if God were perched on our kitchen ceiling, listening.

"Magda Lupescu proved," Grandpa would say, as much to God as to us, "that a Jewish girl could become the Queen of Romania!"

• • •

34
THAT SUNDAY

Spring 1940. Even as war sweeps across Europe, most people think of Romania, if they think of it at all, as a musical comedy country. But this Romania, rich in natural resources and giddy from decades of prosperity, is no laughing matter.

Hitler knows this. He sees it in the building boom that seeds the boulevards of Bucharest with small Parisian-style skyscrapers. In the oil fields of Ploesti, he sees fuel for the tanks and planes and ships of The Third Reich. In the wheat fields of Transylvania, he sees supper for his soldiers, sailors, and pilots. In Romania's viciously militant Iron Guard, he senses a comrade to be wooed. King Carol is aware, and he knows that however much he struggles to maintain balance, his Romania is a minor player facing the final curtain of an increasingly brutal drama.

Spring 1941. One year later, and Romania is changed, her spine splintered by the nasty weight of the Iron Guard, her spirit smothered. Gaiety is gone. Prosperity is memory. Carol, deposed, has fled with Lupescu, their legendary love usurped by an unholy political romance. Courtship between the Third Reich and the Iron Guard has solidified, thickening into a union so sinister it will suffocate Romania with dread and choke the life out of her Jews.

That year, and over the next, the die is cast. A flood of virulently anti-Semitic measures pours forth on the pages of the official newspaper, *Moniturul Oficial*. Thirty-two laws, thirty-one decrees, and seventeen resolutions eliminate Jews from civil service; limit which professions they can work in: and condemn them to forced labor. Housed in wretched shacks, exposed to cold and hunger, and deprived of medical attention, they dangle on the edge of doom.

Over 200,000 will be stripped of Romanian citizenship, turned into strangers in the land where they were born, for which they fought, and to which they swore allegiance. Deprived of basic rights, with no safe haven or legal option, the Jews of Romania are on dangerous ground in the one place on Earth that they call home.

Iasi, with its large Jewish population, is especially vulnerable. Fearing the worst, many Jews secretly transfer valuables and property to non-Jewish relatives, friends, or neighbors for safekeeping. "We never lived in ghettoes here," I am told. "People always got along, and were eager to help." But good hearts and best intentions are no match for the long reach of armed hatred or the power of calculated treachery.

June 1941. Heat scorches Moldavia with a burning fury. No ordinary heat, but a hotness that dulls the senses and makes reason wither. During that hellish June, "secret" strategies are being finalized. The plan: invade the Soviet Union. Objective: regain the lost province of Bessarabia, seized by the Soviets a year earlier in 1940.

Dictator Ion Antonescu has been in on the plot since January. High-ranking military and civic officials are on board. Tactics are confirmed. Danger hangs heavy in the air. Ordinary citizens sense it. Few know, however, that a subsidiary war is brewing, an equally secret war with a singular, unsuspecting target.

June 19, 1941. Antonescu commands the Ministry of the Interior to observe Jews and track them wherever they go in every province, so that "action can be taken against them when I order it, and when the suitable time comes."

Orders by the Ministry of the Interior are specific to a fault and slavishly followed. Arrest sizeable numbers of Jews in every Moldavian town and hamlet. Acts of hostility, resistance, or disruption are to be punished by death.

General Headquarters heads for the Prut River, which separates Romania from Russia. The First Mobile Detachment of the SSI (Special Information Service), overseers of Antonescu's diabolical scheme, follows close behind. Documents and files on Jews completed earlier by the SSI are concealed inside the detachment's equipment. Joint Romanian-German forces cross the Prut River checkpoint. The invasion of the Soviet Union is underway. The calendar is ripe for disaster.

June 22, 1941. War erupts. Romanian leaders respond by stoking the smoldering embers of ethnic hate. Inciting posters go up on fences and on kiosks, in trams and in trains, and on the walls of public buildings. All fault Jews for the war and demand punishment.

Across the nation, thousands of Jewish men, women, children, and old people are marked for disaster. Expelled from their homes and robbed of their belongings, they are jammed into sealed freight trains: doomed cargo transported to overcrowded work camps where disease, despair, and death await. Nowhere is anti-Semitism more poisonous than in greatly Jewish Iasi.

June 24, 1941. Soviet bombs hit the Rapa Galbena District of Iasi and its cavernous train station. Damage is minimal but rumor is rampant. Soviet parachutists are deployed at the city limits, says the state-run press, and the Jews are working with them. Fueled by panic, many citizens of Iasi are certain that Jews now pose a great and dire threat to public safety.

June 26, 1941. Soviet bombs blast Iasi a second time, wreaking heavy damage to key buildings. Thirty-eight Jews are listed among lives lost in the attack. In the evening paper, General Gheorghe Stavrescu, Commander of the 14th Infantry Division and highest-ranking local military officer, urges the good citizens of Iasi to "help authorities catch our enemies." All fingers of guilt point to the Jews, states Stavrescu. He further warns, "Those in the service of the enemy will be hacked to pieces."

June 27, 1941. Via phone Antonescu orders Colonel Constantin Lupu, commander of the Iasi garrison to: "Cleanse Iasi of its Jewish population." Deferring to files maintained by the SSI, the Iron Guard arrests three Jews. Presumed to be Bolsheviks, they are charged with flashing mirrors from windows to help guide Soviet pilots toward targets within the city; never mind that most bombs are hitting Jewish neighborhoods. Taken away for safekeeping, two of the accused are shot dead by their "guards." The other escapes, disappearing into a cornfield.

Only a few kilometers away, in the little village of Sculeni, Jews are framed for a Romanian-German setback in the Soviet invasion. As punishment, all 315 Sculeni Jews, including women and children, are murdered. The die for Iasi is cast.

June 27. General Stavrescu once more accuses the Jewish population in Iasi of helping the Soviet Air Force. Urging them to "return to legal ways," Stavrescu threatens to kill 100 Jews for every fallen Romanian or German soldier. Finally, he orders Jews to relinquish all telescopes, flashlights, cameras, and film.

That night, in the alleys of Iasi, Iron Guardsmen, armed and aggressive, are heard singing militant marching songs. On the next day, ominous signs begin to appear everywhere. At the Jewish Cemetery, Jewish men are forced to dig large ditches. Soldiers invade Jewish homes, apparently "searching for evidence." Terror is pervasive. Christian houses are marked with crosses. Signs painted on doors read "No Jews Here."

June 28, 1941. Fear paralyzes Iasi. Christian intellectuals and wealthy citizens flee in large numbers. Concerned Christians implore Jewish residents and friends to escape as quickly as they can.

June 28, at night. Six more Jews are arrested on charges of espionage. All are shot dead. In a cunning lie, authorities tell military men and police that Jews have attacked soldiers in the street. The prelude to the pogrom is in full force.

June 28, later that night. Reconnaissance units are deployed to every district. Police are ordered to surrender weapons and not to intervene in "what the army is about to do, regardless of the rights or wrongs of their actions."

The Siguaranta (Security Service) arrests a large number of Jews. All are accused of being left-wing sympathizers and are imprisoned in the basement of the Central Police Station.

June 28. Air-raid alarms sound but not many German planes appear in the sky. One fires a blue flare. This is the signal. Shooting starts. The pogrom begins. In every district of Iasi, pistols blaze bullets and machine gunfire sprays out of houses, from an attic in the university, from Saint Spiridon Hospital, from the building of the State Archives Office.

German soldiers fire shots into the air, at people, at troops marching toward the front, and, in massive profusion, at a column of Romanian soldiers. The battalion fires back with every type of weapon, even 53-millimeter cannons.

Deceitful once again, German soldiers claim that injured and fallen soldiers swell among their ranks due to bedlam instigated by Jews. Yet even as the streets boom with the rat-a-tat of true battle, there is not a shred of proof apparent. No soldier is slain or injured, no weapon is uncovered, not one body discovered, dead or wounded. All the same, both high-ranking Romanian authorities and the public buy into the deception. Panic spreads, and reports of bogus events escalate.

Shooting persists into the night. Then the first "action" is taken. German guardsmen batter their way into Jewish homes. Looking for "evidence," they arrest, pummel, rob, and kill. Patrols of Romanians, lone soldiers, and civilians eagerly join in. Not one rifleman is found in any of the houses.

June 29, 1941. Morning. Surviving Jews are pulled out of their houses and herded toward the center of the city. Some are still in their pajamas and others wear tattered clothing, proof of last night's assault. Many are barefoot, and most are bruised. All are forced to march in unison, hands up to a rhythmic step. To speak is forbidden; even to whisper means death. On they walk, taunted by the crowd lining the street. Ironically these Jews, dazed and frightened and abused, are being taken to the *cestura*, the vast courtyard of the police station, a building dedicated to the employment of justice.

Blatant cruelty and blind hatred transform the crowd on the street into a mob. Spit flies at the Jews. Tears and dirt and mucus stream down their frightened faces. Broken bottles and stones are hurled at them, ripping clothes and gashing skin. Blood gushes from open wounds. Frantic Jews shove each other, trying to take cover in the middle of the marching column. Soldiers on the street bash them with rifle butts. Crazed civilians emerge from their houses, and armed with hoes and spades, hammers, crowbars, and metal rods, they attack. Blows stream down upon the Jews. Many are bludgeoned to death.

At about 1:30 p.m., German soldiers and Romanian police and soldiers surround police headquarters. Stepping over dead bodies in the street, the line of Jews marches on, past trashed shops, their shrieks and moans lost to the roaring crowd, the rattle of firearms, and the insolence of waltzes blasting absurdly from loudspeakers on German motorcars careening through the streets.

At around 2:00 p.m., an air raid siren is heard. More sirens begin to scream. This is the signal. German and Romanian soldiers start to fire right into the crowd. Pistols, machine-guns, automatic arms, and rifles let loose from everywhere: at the steps leading to the Central Police Station, from balconies of neighboring buildings, and from rooftops.

Crazed with fear, several Jews pull down the courtyard fence and try to escape through Union Square. They are shot dead. Others hide in the garden of the adjacent Sidoli Cinema. They are also shot. Soldiers shove their way into houses, again joined by civilians.

On this 29th day of June 1941, "That Sunday," as it will be called, acts of cruelty, suffering, pillage, and murder continue to unfold before unseeing eyes of Romanian civil and military authorities. Some say the street leading to the police station was so slippery with blood that in the *cestura,* the bodies of dead Jews lay stacked like "logs on a road."

Six p.m. No more shots are to be heard. The howling of the mob dies down. German loudspeakers no longer belt out insulting waltzes. Silence falls upon

Iasi. Except for the voice of Major Nicolae Scriban, military judge of the 14th Infantry Division.

Broadcasting over loudspeakers, he commands soldiers to go back to their barracks, and he tells civilians to go home. He orders all doors and windows to be left open. Trucks materialize out of nowhere. Bodies are carted off. The streets are clear of corpses. The next phase of the pogrom is set to begin.

• • •

35
A TERRIBLE DARKNESS

June 30, 1941. Morning. Survivors of the pogrom are taken in haste from police headquarters to the train depot. They are forced to march swiftly, and they are beaten as they walk. Those who cannot keep time—the elderly, the injured, the lame—are shot.

They who get to the square in front of the train station are forced to lie on the ground, face to cement. To speak, or even dare to lift one's head, means instant death. Thieves and pickpockets are brought into the square and let loose among the facedown captives, robbing at will.

Lights from nearby armored vehicles ignite, and the Jews are counted. All are commanded to rise and walk platform to trackside where freight cars wait. Roughly 2,430 Jewish men and women, young and aged, healthy and infirm, are lined up in a row fronting the trains. Soldiers open the doors and push the Jews inside with bayonets and rifle butts. About 150 people are crammed into each car, more than four times the intended capacity. Doors are slammed shut and locked. Air holes are plugged. Motors heat up.

Sealed tight, on this stifling final day of June 1941, the train leaves Iasi bound for the town of Targu Frumos. Boiling heat turns the cars into ovens. Some passengers suffocate. Others go mad. Most vomit. Urine flows like wine. Many shit upon themselves. Some convulse. Others are felled by heart attacks. Or heat stroke. Or they broil to death.

At approximately 7:00 a.m., the doomed train passes through Targu Frumos, which in a stroke of supreme irony, translates as "beautiful village." Neither railway officers nor local authorities think to bring the roasting cars to a halt. Much to his annoyance, the Deputy Commander of the garrison is ordered to stop the train so that the dying and the dead may be unloaded.

Under strict orders, one hundred troops from the railway battalion stand guard over those who managed to live. Jews who beg for water are ignored. Locals who try to help are beaten. Watchful soldiers stop Jews from escaping and shoot any who dare seek water. Piles of bodies in front of the train stew in the simmering heat.

By morning's light, bands of Gypsies are brought to the station and forced to remove the corpses. Surviving Jews are shoved back into the train, which is rerouted to the town of Calarasi.

For six-and-a-half days, Death Train Number One, as it will be called, rides aimlessly back and forth in the hellish heat, passing some stations two or three times on a ride that should take no more than a half-day at most. An insistently cruel sun turns the train into a fire pit with little or no relief for its human cargo.

Sunday, July 6th. Death Train Number One pulls into the station at Calarasi. Of the 2,430 Jews aboard, 1,458 are dead, including two shot trying to escape and several beyond rescue.

Monday, July 7th. Death Train Number Two leaves the Iasi station at about 9 a.m., moving at a snail's pace through the sun-scorched day, and then returning for more prisoners. Blistering heat bakes the wooden wagons. Parched and desperate, passengers drink their own urine to survive. Others suck pus and blood out of their own wounds or devour the sores of those nearby. Some die of asphyxiation. Others go insane. Still others commit suicide. Human flesh cooks.

Eight hours later, on a journey that should take no more than thirty minutes, Death Train Number Two pulls in just outside the little village of Podu Iloaiei. About 1,250 corpses are removed from the cars. Seven hundred and fifty people are still alive. Medical personnel show up.

In Iasi, all is calm again. Officials from numerous civic and government organizations have come to investigate the pogrom. Though findings expose anti-Jewish conspiracy and dire consequence, no one is deemed guilty or held accountable. General Stavrescu, dismissing the entire affair, says, "500 Jewish communists have been murdered in Iasi."

An uncertain civility settles over the city. It dissipates unexpectedly. Military commander, General Dumitru Carlaont, issues a chilling proclamation: Jews are to wear signs to separate them from others. A torrent of similar measures follows. Jews are expelled from their flats. Jews are once more sent to labor camps. Jews are deported, along with the Roma (Gypsies) to Transnistria, a former Soviet area now occupied by Romania.

This is no ordinary deportation but a design for human misery and decease. Thousands are forced to travel by foot in the deadly cold of Balkan winter from Romania to Transnistria. Those who are too weak, too ill, or too lame to keep up the pace are shot. Scores more die of exposure or starvation. Those who make it to Transnistria are housed in what Romanian authorities genteelly call "colonies."

These are no colonies but ghettoes. While not death camps, the barracks of Transnistria achieve the same end in a less structured but equally merciless and effective fashion. Crude, overcrowded shacks with no running water, electricity, or toilets serve as breeding ground for typhus and dysentery.

Romanian Jews are forced to lodge with Russian and Ukrainian Jews. Despite a shared religious ethic, they are culturally different and often do not speak the same language. Marginal rations cause malnutrition and starvation. Romanian and Ukrainian squads mow Jews down in plain sight.

In 1943, King Carol's son Michael stages a successful coup, and expels the Antonescu regime. The nightmare is over, and Romania begins to put the pieces of its national life together again. Seventy thousand Jews return from Transnistria in 1944, only to find themselves at a sad crossroads. They have lost family. They have lost their houses, and they have lost their jobs. They have no place to live. They have no place to work. They ere not yet home and not quite displaced.

The massacre in Iasi is a turning point in the endlessly awful treacheries of the Holocaust: it will serve as a template for future atrocities, teaching the Nazis that one cannot only murder people in front of their own neighbors without resistance but, if the event is properly orchestrated, even enlist neighborly participation. In retrospect, the rest of the world learned something about the human race, and it wasn't such good news.

That Sunday is considered one of the cruelest pogroms in Jewish history. One third of the Jewish population of Iasi perished in the worst way possible, a curious reward for centuries of vibrant cultural and economic contributions.

Why, I wonder, had the facts been so whitewashed in the telling – and by Jews. Perhaps it is selective memory, or maybe because those who told us about it had not lived through it all. Perhaps the shocking facts have been diluted by the healing tides of time.

Maybe, just maybe, it is more than a desire to forget. Maybe the need to look away reflects how deep is the hurt. Greater than the injustice, the unspeakable tragedy, or inconsolable loss, it is a pain that sears the psyche and wounds the soul.

You think you are part of something and you are told, in an instant, that you are not. Someone, unseen and behind closed doors, has determined that you do not have the right to breathe Romanian air, drink Romanian wine, or say "I am a Romanian," which is what you have always said and have always known.

A hidden and armed force, criminal and cunning, has denied your identity and decided that you do not have the right to be who you have always been, live where you have always lived ... or live altogether.

No matter the reasoning: fear, panic, official manipulation, the terrible truth is that those who threw broken bottles and stones at the Jews of Iasi; who struck them with metal bars and beat them to death with hoes and spades; who spat and cursed at them in the ghastly heat of that fatal summer—these same people had earlier danced and joked, worked, studied, lived side by side with, and even wooed and won the very Jews they now tormented. No matter how you view it, the truth of the matter is that these people of Iasi, these soldiers and citizens who now killed Jews, had turned on a dime on those who had been their neighbors, friends, lovers, and workmates, robbing them blow by calculated blow of dignity and life.

Who were these Jews turned into a people apart, thrust into peril, deemed worthy only of mindless abuse, humiliation, and mass murder? These "Jews" were respected members of the community: librarians and historians, artists and models, archers and boxers. They were that nice young photographer who lived down the block, the middle-aged woman who ran the bakery on Main Street, the two sisters who had just opened a beauty parlor, the local school principal.

What of my lost relatives … Haim and Roza? Had good Christian neighbors hidden them, or had their lives drained into the river of Jewish blood that ran red in the streets of Iasi that terrible summer of 1941? What of Monis, and his mystery wife, and their children? Corneliu, Adria, and Gia if those were their names. Had they followed wise advice and fled in the night to safety? Or had they met death on an overheated train to nowhere…? Or dwindled away in a rude barrack, hungry, cold, and broken, and a long way from home.

• • •

PART THREE
THE RETURN

36
ROMANIA REVISITED

*L*a *Multi Ani!* Three words of universal promise, spelled out in marquee bulbs over the main square in Bucharest. *Happy New Year!* Glittery signs, splashy and brash, tell it all, from *La Multi Ani* up above to the Pizza Hut on the corner, garishly dressed in neon and serving American style pizza on the counter and "to go." This Bucharest is a far cry from the struggling city I never got to know twelve years ago. I have returned, as a photographer traveling with the renowned storyteller, Laura Simms. I had shortchanged Bucharest the first time around, so I decided to spend a couple of days on my own before meeting Laura.

It is dark and the city is alive in a way it had not been twelve years earlier. From the bright lights and the lively crowds, you know you are some place special. You are in a big international city with a history. You are somewhere.

I wander into the crisp night, making my way through an imperious but dark and lonely square to the big piazza where bright lights in the sky herald a happy new year.

Walking gingerly past a line of threatening stone pillars, I sense that I am not alone. On cue, a man steps out from behind one of the columns, a tall and slender man in a long coat. Without hesitation, he makes a beeline for me. Lamplight reveals a long angular face framed by a closely cropped dark goatee that says "I am slightly wicked." A glint in his amber eyes completes the picture. Leaning in toward me, he speaks softly in a voice that is low and charged with conspiracy.

"You want girls?"

'No!'

"I can get you girls, beautiful girls, just over from Russia."

"No, no girls."

"You want boys? I can get you boys. Russian Boys. Nice and handsome. Romanian boys, too."

"No! No boys, no girls!" I say, scurrying on, half-smiling.

This was a changed place since my last visit, a place that had gone from somber and scared to unafraid in the boldest sense of the word. The only thing unchanged is my visibility as an American. At home, for as long as I can remember, I am always pegged European. In Europe, I am American, Is it my parka? My haircut? Do I have stars and stripes in my eyes? A few steps farther, into the light and the hustle bustle, and it is apparent that while I remain the same in appearance, Bucharest has changed, and in no small way.

The last time I saw Bucharest she was a city seeking to regain her tattered reputation, a gallant old dame in need of powder and paint and a good hair stylist. This Bucharest is a lady of the moment, ready to dance on tabletops. This is a city in motion, enticingly cosmopolitan, and with a distinctive pulse. You can see it and you can feel it ... everywhere.

Mannequins posture seductively in glitzy shops. Workmen roost on scaffolds, giving welcome facelifts to worn-out villas. Poor and shabby neighborhoods glide unexpectedly into glamorous blocks of honey-colored apartment houses. Over the next few years, this new Bucharest will regain its place as a seat of swank and nightlife, good food and hospitality, and Romania will become one of the fastest-growing economies in Europe.

Laura is here to meet with Ciprian Cobrianu, a dynamic young Romanian actor and her partner in Crystal Camp, a workshop for Romanian orphans where storytelling is to be used as therapy. Ciprian is tall, dark, handsome, and as courteous as he is theatrical. He shares an apartment in Iasi with his brother. It is done up in fetchingly Bohemian style, but too small to house us, he says, and we are to be put up for a few days at the well appointed home of his parents in a nearby town.

The weather is frightening. Arctic winds cut through us, swirling snow blinds us, and much of our way is spent pushing the dying car. Wayside motels are booked to capacity, and we have no choice but to drive till we creep to a halt, get out, push again, and pray. We grin and endure the brutal cold with a high degree of good cheer that sustains us until we reach the cozy warmth of the Cobrianu home.

We are barely in the Cobrianu house when Ciprian's mother says to him, while pointing at us: "I don't know what their nationality is but from the smiles on their faces, they must be Romanian." Then she feeds us.

"I am going to serve you something," she says, "that you have never eaten before, I am sure. It is called... mamaliga!"

You could hear our shrieks in New York.

"I was brought up on mamaliga," says Laura. Mamaliga always evaded my childhood, but my family talked about it so much that I might as well have been brought up on it. Mention "mamaliga" and bells go off in my cells.

"What does your house look like?" Ciprian's father asks me. I try to describe the small frame Victorian in Syracuse, New York, which looks like it belongs in San Francisco. "It is attached to other houses on the street, and is what we call a row house. Old houses in a row."

He nods, impressed. "There is a little porch with a little garden in the front," I continue.

He smiles a smile of wonder and delight.

"And the whole house is painted blue," I say proudly.

Floored by the notion of such a thing, Mr. Cobrianu ponders it a moment. "If it's your house," he concludes, "it must be beautiful."

We eat and we drink and we eat some more, and then gastronomic history repeats itself. Ciprian's mother brings to the table a boiled-fish-and-aspic dish, that same suspect dish-with-no-name that Grandma used to make for Grandpa.

"You don't have to eat that if you don't want to," Ciprian says, seeing the look of utter horror on my face.

"You don't understand, Ciprian. This is my childhood coming back to haunt me."

Next day we call on neighbors. Christmas is around the corner, and baskets of apples stand next to each door to ensure wishes for good health and good luck in the New Year.

On the road again, endless snow turns the world ghostly and merciless wind makes driving dangerous. We are heading back to Iasi to pick up Ciprian's good friend, a social worker named Danielle. A string of headlights emerges out of the fierce and windy landscape around us, forging an uncertain path on a barren white road flanked by rows of leafless trees.

After a day or two in Iasi, we will go to Bukovina to stay with Danielle's parents and to visit peasant cousins of hers in the country. Once again we stop to eat at a snazzy roadside café that could hold its own on Rodeo Drive. Stores along the way are stocked with well-packaged, high-priced gourmet foods and trendy merchandise. "Who can afford all of this?" I ask.

"Before the Revolution," says Danielle, "there were people here with money but there was nothing to buy. Now there is plenty to buy but no one can afford it!" That, I think to myself, is the better part of capitalism: people will work hard to buy, save, borrow, and maybe even steal.

Snow has not stopped falling. Giant evergreens line the hills along the road, needled branches crusted with crystal. We are passing through Maramuresc. This is an area famed for its passionate refusal to comply with Ceausescu's design for stripping Romania of its culture. Old Romania is everywhere.

Villages glitter in sunlit snowy valleys, proof again of how enchanted is the light in this part of the world. After the hills come wide fields of ice and white. Occasional arches appear, curiously Asian in feel and eerily isolated, like gateways to nowhere. One can only wonder who passed through these lone entryways, when, where they were going, and what once lay beyond.

Wind sweeps through silver hills. Coffee by the fire in a toasty country wayside stop works wonders, before taking on the snow-cold world once more. Down a bend in the road, spires and rooftops rise above the heads of a rowdy crowd encircling a group of local performers. We hear odd tinkling music, a kind of rhythmic trample punctuated by drumbeats, and the sound of feet crunching packed snow in a deliberate militant tempo. Ciprian whispers to me "Hold on to your wallet." I transfer my wallet to my front pocket, as we make our way, pushed and pulled by the crowd, for a front row look at a standing-room-only show.

Dressed up in spangled, fanciful costumes, young men talk-sing their way through the Romanian folk tale about a bear and stag, while stomp-dancing to the jangle of tambourines, an occasional flute, and the hypnotic thumping of drums. Moving as a group, they strut their stuff in front of one house, chant and prance emphatically, and then move on. House to house they go, and at each stop, spirited neighbors come out and stuff the dancers with Christmas treats to eat and drinks to wash it down. Lots of drinks. They drink and they drink till, I am told, they can no longer stand up straight. Which we can see happening.

Christmas Eve falls upon Maramuresc, and women in black come out of church. Walking in stately measured procession, each holds a single thick-lit candle in her hand. A sense of age-old tradition, of medieval pageantry somber and otherworldly, haunts the crisp night air. Candles flicker in the dark. Snow, lustrous and feathery, drifts down and down from high heaven to earth. Ice shimmers. Romania is famous for cold and bitter winters, but we are about to live through one of the most ferocious winters of the twentieth century.

Next stop Suceava, where we will stay with Danielle's parents.

"They are simple, hard working people," she says, "and they love their children." They are also warm and gracious. Making your own bed is forbidden. Food is a constant and mamaliga is served morning, noon, and night; hot, cold, main dish, and side. Their apartment is pleasant with the obligatory breakfront in the living room filled with dishware and bric-a-brac, and a terrace off the living room is used to store firewood for the stove. Good thing, too. It is cold, and with hot water at a premium, we bathe every three days. "I feel so dirty," Laura confides.

"Before the Revolution," Danielle says, "the buses ran on time and we had hot water regularly but people were afraid to open their mouths. You could be taken away in the middle of the night for the wrong word overheard. Now everyone says whatever they want but nothing runs on time and we don't have hot water."

To battle the icy morning, Danielle's father urges us to swill down a glass of horinca, a kind of twice-brewed plum version of vodka. One sniff and I am scandalized at the thought of drinking such strong stuff so early in the morning. By the second day, I can't wait. This is fuel, I realize, and the only way to beat the chill of day, and as I think this, memories of my grandfather belting down shots of whisky in winter came to mind. One swift swallow emptied his shot glass, followed by a grateful "aahhhhhhhhhh."

Christmas Day. The weather is frosty, but the place is warm, comforting, and suddenly filled with the sound of distant song. Such heavenly voices that I am certain angels are singing in the hallway. Not too far from the mark, the voices belong to two priests. Making their way through the building, they sing as they go, blessing each home in blissful tones.

Radiating good will, the priests enter our apartment bearing smiles as sweet as their voices. I have no intention of photographing them, certain it would be an intrusion. But the older of the two insists that I take their picture. "I am the priest," he says, in English, with a devilish grin, and then points to his sidekick. "And this one," he adds, "He is my collaborator!!!!"

A similar incident happens when we visit Ciprian's grandparents. In their village local priests go from house to house, stopping in for cakes and tea and a bite to eat, an obvious honor for the chosen household. The two priests we meet are younger in age than those in the apartment of Danielle's parents. Their manner is soothingly sedate and they dress in traditional long dark robes. Ciprian cautions me against taking their photos, which, as it turns out, makes his grandmother unhappy.

Ciprian's grandparents are non-Jewish versions of my grandparents, and I am convinced that we are bound by something Romanian, or maybe genetically universal. His grandfather, handsome and hale and silver haired, is a born storyteller, eloquent and with a wry sense of humor just like my grandpa. His grandmother is energetic, possessed of abundant good will, and a great cook just like my grandma. And she can't stop pinching her grandson's cheeks, which embarrasses him.

According to Ciprian's grandfather, the local papers report that the Prime Minister of Romania recently visited Israel, where Romanian Jews besieged him telling him they wanted to come back.

"Would they be welcome, if they came back, if it were feasible?" I ask.

"With open arms," he answers. "The Jews were so dynamic. They got things done for the country. The non-Jews are smart enough to do it, but they're too busy fighting with one another. And I will tell you something about Jews," he says, a twinkle in his eyes. "If a Jewish friend or neighbor lent you money he didn't just give the money to you, he made sure you invested it wisely!"

The grandmother can't stop feeding us, and her food is wonderful but different from the Romanian food I know, probably because of the region. Chicken soup is carpeted with fresh cut parsley and packed with red peppers. Red peppers in my grandmother's cooking were a colorful side dish, tossed with vinegar and oil and baked or broiled. But here red peppers are a culinary mainstay, served with mamaliga, cooked in soups and stews, and sprinkled on salads.

A big chimney dominates the kitchen. Tiled in rich brown ceramic, and rising from floor to ceiling, it decorates and heats the spacious room. This kind of chimney appears in all the houses we've been in, and Laura drops down on the floor in front of it, leans back, and warms herself. "Our grandparents lived in houses like this," she said. I was thinking the same.

Our game plan, in fact, is to see our ancestral towns which are not that far apart. We plan to visit Dorohoi where Laura's family came from, and I would get to revisit Stefanesti. Laura assures me that with her at the helm, we will not be shy about meeting the Gypsies who live in the house where once my grandmother lived. But nature it turns out has other ideas, and days on end of stormy snow and wind make travel to the countryside impossible.

What a disappointment. I had envisioned us knocking on the door of the house on Strada Noroba Guiler. Slowly, the door would open, and I would get to see where my grandmother grew up. See the kitchen where Gunnar, her pet goose, ate off the table with the rest of the family, and the parlor where the neighbors came to pay their respects after her father died. Laura is concerned that I am disappointed, and I tell her not to worry, knowing that she is as dismayed as I am. It is just one of those things. There is nothing to be done except to trudge on, get out, push the car, and pray for the best along a windy, perilously icy, and snowswept path to Iasi.

• • •

37
A CLUE

"**N**o one by your family's name, no one named Grisariu, was born or died in the city of Iasi in the twentieth century."

The voice belongs to Dan Jumara, Director of the Museum of Literature in Iasi, and a respected archivist. Laura has put me in touch with him, and it turns out Dan worked on the Iasi portion of my family search, which he describes as "disappointing." We are seated in his office in an ornate university building, and he tells me that all birth and death records in Iasi are now computerized.

A computer search sheds scant but telling light on the whereabouts of my relatives. "No one named Grisariu was born or died in Iasi in the twentieth century," Dan repeats. "Your uncle must have lived elsewhere."

Monis and his family had not lived in Iasi. Great-Grandma Sura had not died there either. Haim and Roza, with whom Sura lived, must also have moved elsewhere.

Grandma said that after the death of her father, her older brothers packed the family up and moved them from Stefanesti to Iasi. I figured they had all moved together: Sura, the matriarch; Grandma, age 12 or so; Haim and Monis, whom I imagined as teen boys; and Uncle Mauritz, a toddler. All moving to Iasi as a family unit. Now it appears that Monis, the oldest, might have struck out on his own years before. I am not convinced.

"It was the 1880s, I don't think people moved around that much."

"On the contrary, there were railroads and horse-drawn carriages, and Romania was prosperous then. If your uncle had an opportunity to work in a village or city anywhere else in the country, he would have taken advantage of it. After all, your grandfather went to London!"

Dan was right. Monis was the oldest, and based on Great-Grandma Sura's age, he could have been as much as ten years older than my grandmother. People married much younger then, and it was not unusual to lose children to diseases that have all but disappeared today or are better treated. This would explain the big gap in age between Monis and the others, and it is probable that he married and moved away years before the rest of the family went to Iasi.

What a breakthrough. Monis lived in another town or city. He and his family were not present in Grandma's memories. Haim, however, lived in the same household, so he and later Roza would have been active in Grandma (and Grandpa's) young life.

In an era of limited communication when the telephone had not yet been invented, it is probable that Grandma barely knew Monis's wife, and she might not have ever met their children, her nieces and nephew. More than likely their names were lost in time, consumed by the passing years and miles, and those twists of fate and demands of life that fall upon us all.

There was also the chance that Monis and his family emigrated to another country. In truth, I sensed that such a move would have been newsworthy, the stuff of mention, as with the oft-cited Cousin Chaimeril who went to Argentina, and even a handful of lesser-known cousins who landed in Canada.

Furthermore, all Jews we spoke to in Romania refuted the idea of our relatives moving away altogether. Progress and modernity defined Romania in the twentieth century and the country was riding high. Life was agreeable, they explained. All agreed it unlikely that anyone would have left between the two world wars.

True, I hadn't a notion as to where Monis lived, even what the names of his wife and children were, or what had happened to them during the Holocaust. But this is a beginning. Knowing that they hadn't lived in Iasi is enough to explain their absence, no less their lack of identity in my grandmother's stories and in her life.

Over the ensuing few years, I would search news groups and websites ... without much luck. I uncover a few Grisarius in Israel, but my e-mails draw frost. All are uniformly too young to know anything, or to care. "Before my time," one young Grisariu replies. "But I'll run it by my father, when he comes home." I never heard from him again. I scour Romanian telephone books and write to a handful of Grisarius, mostly in the area of Botosani. No response.

At a loss and scrambling for ideas, something comes to mind, something I had noticed while in the cemetery at Stefanesti. A few tombstones bore the name "G-r-i-s-a-r-u" rather than G-r-i-s-a-r-i-u. This was almost identical in spelling to ours, but minus the last "i." On a hunch, I do a name search on AOL. Several Grisarus surface. I contact them all, and one answers. Marc Grisaru, a scientist at MIT.

At that time I thought that Uncle Monis came from Iasi and I told Marc I was looking for information on Monis Grisariu of Iasi and his descendants. He says that his father had business dealings in Iasi, and were he still alive he might be of help. But he goes on to say that his family didn't come from Iasi. During the war, he tells me, they lived in Bucharest, but originally they came from a small town called...Stefanesti.

"My grandmother came from Stefanesti!"

Marc tells me that there was still a family named Grisariu in the town when he lived there, spelling their name the way we did, and that they were cousins to his family.

This is a triumph that could only be accomplished in the age of the Internet. There we are, distant cousins, many times removed and worlds apart, touching base through cyberspace. Marc also says that I am not the first person to contact him in search of familial clues. So there are other Grisarius, or relatives of Grisarius, out there looking, but I have yet to find them, and they have not yet found me.

Star genealogists Gary Mokotoff and Eileen Pollack conduct an annual Jewish genealogy workshop in Salt Lake City, working with the Mormon Family Library, one of the most extensive genealogical archives in the world. I sign on for what turns out to be a wonderful trip and a terrific learning experience. There would be, however, a hitch for me, and I could feel it in my genealogical bones.

Most of my fellow researchers have roots in Russia and Poland. Under Gary and Eileen's guidance, they sit happily chained to computers, in the research room dedicated to Eastern Europe. One by one, they strike genealogical gold. Records from these countries are extensive and available on microfilm and via the Internet. What's more, Russia and Poland employ a patronymic naming system. This means that the middle name reveals the prior generation, i.e., David Mihailovich followed by the surname, would translate as David, son of Mihail. No such luck in my neck of the genealogical woods.

Forget about an obliging naming system. Romania does not even microfilm its archives. My colleagues get two generations for the price of one. I get zilch. Outside of a few print volumes written in Romanian, which no one could translate, there is no documentation present of any sort in any media. Romania remains cloaked in mystery. There is nothing to research.

Gary makes it clear that my situation with Monis is the proverbial "needle in a haystack." Monis might have settled anywhere in Romania, so I would have to travel to or contact, every town hall and every municipal archive within Romania proper. This is the only way to find out where he lived, how he earned his living, where his children had been born and their names, and what fate held in store for that entire leg of the family. It is a thorny task, if not impossible, that turns Salt Lake into a socially pleasant but genealogically futile excursion for me. What to do?

First I tour the Great Salt Lake. Then I ride the city's smashing light rail system. Day one takes me through spectacular hills to the University of Utah. Day two, I zoom along a different route to a suburb appropriately called Sandy.

I explore the city's architecturally stunning, award-winning downtown Library. I visit the surprisingly forward thinking Museum of Art. I drink gallons of coffee at the Starbucks in the Marriott Hotel. By day four I realize all is not lost, and so I decide to attack the voluminous resources in the British Section of the Mormon Family Library to see if I can find out anything about the Cohens of Redmans Road.

My fellow researchers are jealous. While they plow through records in impenetrable Polish and unfathomable Russian, I get to work in an area where everything is transcribed in impeccable English. Say what you will, I'll always have London.

At one point in my British research, one of the helpful Mormon elders takes me aside.

"Pardon me, this Cohen family you are researching, are they Jewish?"

"What makes you think that?" I am tempted to answer but instead offer a polite "yes."

He is getting ready to work on a study of Jewish families in London in the early twentieth century and asks if I could provide him with my family's history for possible inclusion. I am thrilled, and I promise to write with all the details of our family life in London, once I get home.

My fellow researchers continue on, shackled to their computers, treating me to discourses of triumph over dinner. I have no such victories but in the British section I would find that perseverance is its own reward; that the past surrenders its secrets when least expected, and that once unleashed those secrets multiply.

• • •

38
GOLDIE

A breakthrough. I have been conducting a triple-edged genealogical search. First, looking for missing relatives in Romania. Second, trying to locate the grave of Goldie Cohen, the daughter my grandparents lost in England. Lastly, attempting to document my grandparents' arrival in America.

In Salt Lake, I had managed to locate Goldie's death certificate and ordered a copy, but I cannot make headway locating where she is actually buried. Switching gears I begin to concentrate on specifics of our family in London, only to stumble upon a mystery every bit as haunting as that of our Balkan past.

Goldie Cohen died, her death certificate reads, "of smoke and shock caused by her clothes igniting whilst playing with matches during the absence of her mother." *During the absence of her mother*, such an accusatory phrase, so sobering, that even reading those words I feel the same sorrow now my grandmother felt then, regret that would course through her veins for the rest of her life.

"Plying with matches?" *Playing with matches* does not conform to what I know to be the truth. Little Goldie had been given to dancing, they had all said. Dancing in her little long dress that reached almost to the floor, in the fashion of the day. She had been left in the care of a neighbor boy while her mother/my grandmother went to the corner store to buy a bottle of milk, an errand so commonplace it did not merit mention.

In those few stolen moments little Goldie danced her way around the room, dressed up in her mother's/my grandmother's shawl - or was it a scarf - as she loved to do. Whirling about, and waving the hem of her little long dress, as only she could, Goldie neared the hearth and danced her way into a fiery death. That is what Grandma told me. That is what my mother told me. That is what Aunt Lily said. At different times, in different places, that is what they all knew to be the truth.

Cousin Norman might have answers. He is Aunt Betty's oldest son, and she would have been four or five at the time it happened; surely such a dreadful moment would have lingered in her memory. Were there any anecdotes about Goldie that Betty recalled, I ask in the note, any recollections or reflections on what had happened? All questions I had never thought to ask my Aunt Betty when she was alive.

Norman writes back. His mother had remembered Goldie, he says, as a "gay, lively child who loved to dance," and there is more. On that crisp afternoon in a late London autumn, when Goldie danced, her older siblings, Betty and Jack, were in school. Summoned home, they returned to a house turned inside out by unexpected tragedy and inconsolable grief.

Goldie caught fire in the fireplace, Betty had said, while dancing in her little long dress. Whether out of fright or foolishness, the neighbor boy who was watching her took to his heels and ran out of the room, slamming the door behind him. Norman thinks he was backward, or not quite right. That could have been rumor stemming from the fact that he was not in school with the other children, or it might have been a known truth, or fiction born of gossip. We will never know.

Rising smoke and the sharp sound of the parlor door banging shut made Uncle Zeidel rush downstairs from his apartment above. He threw himself against the door and battered it open, but Goldie was beyond help.

Who knew how accurate little Goldie's death certificate is in its report of her awful end. It is to the eye an appropriately, eerily, delicate paper with little space for words to describe cause of death. Who will ever know what really happened?

Perhaps Goldie had played with matchsticks while dancing, and whirling about, had caught on fire in a blaze incited by lit matches.

Perhaps there was simply not enough space on the certificate to go into such terrifying detail. Perhaps not.

Maybe *this* is the truth. Maybe Goldie did nothing more than play with matches, industriously striking one against the other, as a child might, and in that way she did catch fire. Just a little girl playing with matches, "in the absence of her mother."

There is another possibility. Maybe little Goldie persuaded the backward boy to dance with her and as they whirled about the room her dress caught fire. Or perhaps she tripped and tumbled into the flames. Or maybe the dancing boy tossed her into the fire in a fit of simple-minded excess. Or could it be that something primitive and mean surfaced within him, between them. Worse things have happened in this world.

There is a less sensational explanation, one that lingers in the mind and haunts the heart. Maybe, just maybe, Goldie's love of dancing had over the years woven its way into the telling of her sad demise, and a new truth grew out of it, the way a story told and retold, with time, takes on a life of its own.

On an earlier trip to England, I had gone to the East End to look for the house that my grandparents shared with Zeidel and Yetta. Forty-five Redmans Road turns out to be one of a line of quaint row houses fronting handsome Stepney Green. All are intact, except for No. 45. Its ground floor, where once my grandparents lived, had been turned into a storefront.

On that trip I also found Yetta's grave. It was an easy adventure given that a post-card of the burial site, complete with a photo of the stone and the cemetery address, had survived over the years in our house.

Edmonton Cemetery is located in what would have been suburban London in 1909. Yetta's stone appears more modest in person than in the photo we had. It is a simple momument inscribed with one single word: "Mum." I place a small rock, a token of visitation and remembrance, on the rim of my great-aunt's gravestone.

I ask the man in the office if he can find any record of Goldie Cohen, presuming that she would have been buried in the same cemetery as Yetta. He picks up an ancient book and proceeds to examine its crinkly pages with care. Running a stubby finger over columns of handwritten entries, he repeatedly shakes his head "no."

Well, if nothing else, I had done right, and I felt a great and moving warmth surge through me. I had paid homage to my grandparents' earlier world. Later my mother would tell me that my grandparents and Yetta didn't get along, squabbling over the way the house was run, who fed the workers, how finances were conducted, and why what was done when.

I had given up hope of finding Goldie's grave when I stumbled upon a London Children's Cemetery. Its gates are locked, and this is my last day in England. Time is running out. I scale the wall that rings the cemetery, looking from one small grave-stone to another. She was nowhere to be found.

A friend suggests that perhaps Goldie's grave had been destroyed during the Blitz, but even if that were so, a record of its location has to exist. This is not Balkan Europe too many years ago, or a continent set aflame by what would justly be called a Holocaust. London in the 20th century. Goldie's grave has to be somewhere. Yet it might as well be nowhere.

Call it sentiment, a yearning born of steeping myself in the past, or the romantic consequence of assuming the mantle of family archivist, but I want to place a stone on Goldie's gravestone, put flowers on the ground above her, pay tribute to a little long-lost golden girl whose dreadful death paved the path of our family's future. Yet her final resting place is as sealed in secrecy as that of the relatives in distant Romania.

Discovering Goldie's death certificate is an achievement in a family whose past consistently evades documentation. For a people of little fame and less fortune, my family's past seems to be locked away in mysterious places. Even immigration records, so accessible through genealogy websites, prove a challenge.

Grandpa had arrived in America months before Grandma, as was the custom, to scope out the new land and to seek work and a place to live. But finding information on him is daunting: the sheer numbers of men named Abraham Cohen landing in New York City during the great wave of immigration in the 1900s is staggering. Grandma's passage to America is equally elusive, but after endless hours of scouring the Internet documentation on her arrival to New York surfaces.

She had brought Jack and Betty with her, I knew, and they had come tourist class and docked uptown. Distinguishing details, to be sure, but more difficult to trace than the standard entrance through Ellis Island. What is really problematic is Grandma's first name. In England, she had reinvented herself by changing her birth name, Chaia Basa, to the Anglican Clara. Yet her documents carried her name from Romania misspelled as Chaje Basie.

Chaia/Chaje/Clara Cohen came over on the steamer St. Paul, the records state, with two children, Jake and Betty. Jake, born Iancu in Romania, known as Jacob in England, was not yet Jack. Betty, born Rebecca in England, nicknamed Becky, had transformed herself later on into the popular Jazz Age "Betty."

More than likely a harried immigration officer misheard Becky as Betty and Jacob as Jake. None of which matters given the stunning dates of my grandmother's coming to America, surviving children in hand … dates haunted by cryptic notions of tragedy and consequence.

Goldie Cohen died in London on November 28, 1908. Her mother/my grandmother landed in America on November 29, 1909, almost one year later to the day.

• • •

There is something else, something one can't describe precisely, abstract yet corporeal, ethereal yet profound. If Goldie had not perished so terribly, my grandparents would have stayed in England. Why would they have left where they had been so prosperous and proud? Our family would have been British. We would have all been different, other than we were. I would not have been born as I am.

If Yetta had not gone up in flames, Zeidel would not have left England only to die in America. One never knows, but it is likely that in the absence of such turmoil, his children's lives would have been less tattered, less troubled, and certainly more stable.

Grandma and Grandpa. Zeidel and Yetta. Their children. Their children's children. These were the people whose dreams and defeats, valor and folly, laughter and tears echoed silently within the walls of the house where I grew up. I was the one who heard them, a silent witness to the theater of their lives. I had unearthed their stories. Our stories. Stories screaming to be told, yearning to be heard.

• • •

39
FOUR COUSINS

"**I** remember where they slept!" The voice belongs to my mother. She is talking about Zeidel's children, after they left the orphanage and came to stay with my grandparents. "A neighbor upstairs kept a spare room for relatives from Europe, and that's where the boys slept. Their sister, Annie Dinkles, stayed with Tante ChaRussa."

Their sister, Annie Dinkles. Somehow I had never made that connection, that Annie Dinkles was actually Zeidel's daughter Annie, the girl cousin from London.

A neighbor upstairs ... that's where the boys slept. Are there people like that today? I thought to myself. So generous, giving, and selfless. There are such people, I am sure, among each successive wave of immigrants ... among Asians, Latinos, and Africans today. When we are lower down on the economic ladder, and strangers in a strange land, we do more for each other because we need each other more.

Basking in memory, Mom begins to reminisce about the boy cousins who lived with Grandma and Grandpa. Benny, oldest of the boys, was a prizefighter. Then came Davy who was hardly remembered, and Joseph, forever remembered as Gentleman Jim, the black sheep.

Mom remembers being fascinated by seeing Benny shadow-box in the hall. Grandpa was less than impressed with ringside Benny, but for practical reasons. "Benny," he used to say, "they'll bring your bones home in a bag of cement." But nobody brought Benny's bones home in a bag of cement. Instead, he went up the river on a Hudson River day cruise, fell out of the boat, down into the water, and drowned.

His brothers, Davy and Gentleman Jim, went another route. Both, in their own ways, became wild boys of the road, like the heroes in adventure books. Davy ran away in the late 1920s. No word of his whereabouts! After a decade of looking, someone in the family managed to find him. Davy Cohen was a radio announcer in Lincoln, Nebraska.

"Lincoln, Nebraska!" I exclaimed. "Lincoln, Nebraska! Maybe Chicago, maybe Minneapolis, but Lincoln, Nebraska! You'd have to work hard to make that one up."

Gentleman Jim outdid Davy, and his story was sheer escapade, the stuff of a weekly TV series, and family legend. Everyone agreed that Gentleman was a brilliant, sensitive boy but with an eccentric streak. My mother remembered that he had a photographic memory, which he put to good use at parties. Grandma remembered finding him on the fire escape at night, quoting poetry to the world at large, and when she bought him new shoes, surely at great sacrifice, he threw those Thom McAn's out the kitchen window.

Gentleman was also given to writing poetry, and a moving snippet of his work survives in my mother's high school autograph book. That was penned in 1934, the year she graduated. By 1935, Gentleman had run away, like his brother before him. By 1938, he had been found. No one would ever tell me what had happened, or how he came to be called Gentleman Jim. But when I was very little, I overheard some of my mother's cousins talking.

"You let him into your house?"

"How could you?"

"He's so dirty!"

I wonder how Gentleman Jim had gotten so dirty, and why he was so scorned.

Years later, Uncle Jack spilled the beans.

"Jeffrey boy, one day I got a call, and you won't believe this, from the authorities in the State of Georgia."

My uncle was right. Gentlemen's story was a lulu. On the loose in the Deep South, he had been picked up for vagrancy. He was serving time on a Georgia chain gang, and he had given Uncle Jack's name as a reference.

Our cousin, Joseph Cohen, son of a prosperous British cooper, had become an authentic Depression-era hobo, one of the hordes of poor or homeless men who rode the rails in those days, seeking work or shelter or a new life somewhere, somehow. It was with tongue in cheek that they called him Gentleman Jim, I believe, because he was the opposite. Or maybe it was because of the poetry he wrote.

Appropriately, the tale of his wanderings had more than the touch of a poet about it. Using his photographic memory as a tool for survival, he would ferret out lone synagogues in small towns in Iowa, Kentucky, Mississippi, or wherever. He'd see what portion of the scriptures they were reading that week, commit it to memory, then pawn himself off as a Biblical scholar. Applauded as a learned man from God-knows-where, he'd be welcome, sheltered and fed, and, I would expect, matched with somebody's eligible daughter.

By my time Gentleman Jim was long out of the picture, but I sure knew who he was. He may have been talked about, sneered at, and disdained but he had become the central figure in one of our most colorful and enduring family stories.

I am fourteen when Gentleman Jim appears at our door, carrying in his hands a box of Loft's cordial cherries. He remembered how much Grandma loved those sweet chocolates with the syrupy cherry centers, "almost as much as she loved cherry vanilla ice cream," he tells me, beaming broadly. What a kindly looking man this lost cousin is, for all his woes. He looks a little like my Uncle Jack, only not quite as handsome. He is slightly paunchy, breaks into a radiant smile whenever he sees me, and of all things, he wears a suit and tie.

Gentleman Jim is happy to see us, but no one is happy to see him. With his rumpled shirt and slightly soiled tie, he is a little the worse for wear. This aggravates Grandma no end, and Grandpa accepts him only begrudgingly as a live partner in pinochle.

Uncle Jack comes over to tell Gentleman to leave before my mother's latest date, a promising underwear salesman from Baltimore, comes to call, and I make sure to keep my friends away. After all, this man is a black sheep.

Mom commented on the irony of it all. Those orphan cousins from London really owe Grandma and Grandpa for what they did for them, she said, and only Gentleman comes around to visit. It is true.

Maybe Gentleman doesn't live up to everybody's standards, but he is the only person in the family who gives me a junior high school graduation present. A Timex watch. I keep it for years and from time to time I look at the watch, and I think of Gentleman Jim and how good-natured he was, and I feel badly that I had not been kinder to him.

He left us after that visit, taking off on what would be his final journey. Joseph Cohen aka Gentleman Jim died heading north on the Taconic State Parkway. It was said that a heart attack did him in, or maybe his heart had been damaged by life. Only three people went to his funeral: his sister Annie, my mother, and my Aunt Betty.

• • •

40

LONDON
REVISITED

I have England on my mind, and for the second time in my life, I am London bound. Following in the footsteps of my mother, Aunt Betty, and Cousin Norman, I set out—as I had on the earlier trip—to visit the house my grandparents shared with Zeidel and Yetta: 45 Redmans Road.

It has been two decades, and at this point I don't really know where I'm going. I do know that Redmans Road is in the East End, and I am convinced that Mile End Station is my destination. Why not? Mile End is a name engraved on my grandfather's old bankbook, which somehow survived the years, turning from a practical item for Cohen Brothers Cooperage in London into a curio in Brooklyn. Mile End is also a stop on the tubes in the East End, so I am sure that getting off here will get me where I want to go.

I see quaint Victorian houses. I see a stately red brick library, and I even see St. Mary-le-Bow's Church. According to London tradition, to be a true cockney one has to be born within the sound of the Bow bells. Had my grandparents lived in this neighborhood their children would have been honest-to-goodness cockneys.

Redmans Road is nowhere in the vicinity of those fabled bells. A kind stranger tells me that I am a slight ways off from where I ought to be which is the Stepney Green station. The good news is I can get there by foot.

Mile End Road turns into a long, long stream of stalls and carts, and open-air marts where energetic merchants hawk everything from electronics to packaged and fresh foodstuffs, and armies of shoppers bargain and fuss over bolts of cloth and shiny trinkets, cut-rate clothing and cell phones.

To my surprise, London Hospital rises into view, its aura of gravity and purpose enhanced by weathered brick and imposing scale. This is a building that means business. Set back from Mile End by a grand staircase, it casts a sobering eye upon the clatter of the street below and the ceaseless chatter of voices born in Pakistan and India, in the Middle and Far East. In my grandparents' day, sounds of Eastern Europe filled the air.

Looking up and down this endlessly busy street, I can feel the summer day around me begin to evaporate. A grey fog rolls in, uninvited, and August slowly drifts into November, an autumn day long ago when fate reshaped my family's future.

I can see my grandmother, little Goldie by her side, coming up the street. How straight she stands and how fine she looks. Oh, Grandma, were you ever that young? I watch her lean down to Goldie, on this, the last day of Goldie's life, and I overhear her say, "Let us go visit Papa." I can see the child's face brighten at the prospect of seeing her father/my grandfather, who is in the hospital recovering from an appendectomy.

Going to London Hospital! I had always envisioned Grandma with her hair piled high upon her head, topped by those big hats that women wore then, and Goldie by her side, blond curls tucked under a velvet cap. My grandmother taking her little daughter on a streetcar or maybe riding the tubes to go to London Hospital "to see Papa."

But London Hospital stands only a few blocks from Redmans Road, and my notion of a streetcar vanishes. Now Goldie and her mother/my grandmother walk to the hospital down a grey and foggy street in London on the cusp of winter, a long time ago.

That Goldie was the darling of the day, the golden girl, I had no doubt. She must have been fetching. Grandma remembered that while they were visiting Grandpa, a nurse was so taken with Goldie that she offered to take care of her, freeing my grandmother to go about the chores of the afternoon. She would, she had said, bring Goldie back to the hospital when day was done. "How could I leave my child in the care of another person?" Grandma said to me. It was too bad she hadn't.

Lost in thought, I wander unaware past Stepney Green, where I ought to be, and into adjacent Whitechapel. Cousin Norman and I figured that this was where our grandparents settled. Had they lived here, their children/my aunts and uncle would have grown up in a crowded slum packed with Russian Jews and Irishmen.

Likened to New York City's Lower East Side, Old Whitechapel had also been described as "worse than anything in Russia." Worse yet, its cobbled alleys once drew scarlet fame as the stomping grounds of Jack the Ripper. Today it seems merely crowded and very seedy. Walking out of Whitechapel, I finally turn off the main street onto Stepney Green and Redmans Road.

On my first visit to England, I found Numbers 45-51 Redmans Road and took it in stride. How handsome these houses still are, I had thought, and they were nearly new when my grandparents had lived here.

Ironically the row of brick houses was miraculously intact, except for Number 45. I knew my grandparents lived on the first floor, and Zeidel and Yetta had lived upstairs. That the ground floor of Number 45 had been remodeled into a store did not faze me in the least. I looked, I saw, I took a picture. I felt nothing. I was like a schoolboy on a field trip for a social studies class.

Twenty years later I am back again, this time with a two-pronged plan. First, I am determined to find Goldie's gravesite, and I have done my homework. In the months before departure, I scour British Jewish cemetery websites, but her name never comes up. I e-mail the Federation of London Synagogues, the archives in Tower Hamlin Library, the London Jewish Museum, and one or two "experts" on Jewish Genealogy in the United Kingdom, and even a Mormon contact left over from Salt Lake City. Some respond with polite yet vague answers, another indicates promise eventually unfulfilled, and others do not answer at all.

Undeterred, I concentrate on phase two of the plan: my grandparent's house. I will enter the storefront at Number 45, introduce myself, explain the purpose of my visit, and ask to tour the inside. I want to see the fireplace, the fatal fireplace that twice took a swipe at our family's fate. Very possibly it is still present.

There is a hitch. Since my last visit Numbers 45-51 have fallen prey to the bull-dozer. New buildings stand in their stead, and Number 45 where once my grandparents lived and thrived is a youth hostel. Now strangers, students, old hippies, and frugal tourists joke and smoke and place their heads on a British pillow for a night's sleep on the cheap. I could have slept here!

Unable to look at the youth hostel any longer, I turn away. How perfectly preserved the rest of the street is, and how gracefully the crescent of Redmans Road wraps about Stepney Green. This is what my grandparents saw every day when they left the house. Grandma going to market or to the dressmaker. Grandpa loading barrels onto a wagon or taking the children to Piccadilly on Sunday, which he always talked about. I peer across the Green and into their past world. From behind cross-paned windows of 19th century buildings across the way, ghosts of my grandparents' day stare back.

This is the London that might have been ours. Looking up and down Redmans Road, I could see Jack and Betty, as they looked in an old family tintype, now playing on the street with Zeidel's children, Benny, Joseph (who became Gentleman Jim), Davy ,and Annie were long out of the picture when I was growing up, but they were talked about often, and now I see why.

Zeidel's children, and my uncle and aunts lived in the same house then, went to the same school, shared childhood secrets, and surely belonged to the ever present boys and girls clubs which were, I had read, dedicated to "keeping the youth off the street and turning them into fine British citizens and proud Jews." They were more than cousins; they were playmates and childhood pals.

Studying the street map, I find a Jewish cemetery only a few blocks off Stepney Green. All sources indicate that this is an ancient place intended for Sephardic Jews. It predates our time in England and we are not Sephardic, but one never knows.

I follow the map to a fare-thee-well, only to end up at a housing project, and more than once. Directions asked of locals draw blank stares. Trying a different route the next day brings me to a different entrance of the housing project. A third day I fare no better. Where is Goldie?

Wandering back toward the tube stop along Mile End Road, skirting Stepney Green, I look back for a final glance. This is where it all started.

Tears fall not because of what is gone, but because of what my grandparents once had, what they left behind, and never regained. Maybe it was because by the time they moved to America things had changed for them. They were not as young, and they had been wounded by life. Leaving England was not their intent, to be sure, yet Grandma and Grandpa were grateful Americans.

To newcomers in that era America was "the golden land," and my grandparents, like others of their time and class, did everything they could to become as American as possible as quickly as possible. They threw themselves into patriotic extremes with a zeal that bordered on vaudeville. Under the glass of their living room coffee table, they kept a copy of the Declaration of Independence. From their windowsills on Flag Day and on the Fourth of July without fail, flew the Stars and Stripes, and they spouted fractured slang with fearless pride.

Yet for all the Yankee Doodle trimmings, Grandma and Grandpa never forgot Romania or England. One nation gave them birth and made them who they were; the other adopted them and allowed them to become better than they had been. In the recesses of my grandparents' memories, Romania and England became unlikely allies, and the presence of both was tactile in the house where I grew up. And always the rustle of that taffeta dress haunted our collective memory, of Goldie where she danced in unseen corners of our small apartment.

● ● ●

41
PICTURES

"Look at these," says my mother. From a packed closet shelf, she pulls out a box of photos. I had never seen any of these before.

First comes the young woman. She looks at me out of the past, poised but not aloof, at ease in the faded black-and-white world she calls home. Bobbed hair and bow lips place her in the 1920s. Posing before the camera as they did then, she assumes pretense toward glamour, and it suits her well. A blonde aura frames facial features delicate as Dresden china. Awfully dreamy eyes glance upward, beseeching the heavens. Her sleek dress and plump pearls offer a glimpse back at a more elegant era. Such loveliness could have placed her in the movies, a star of the first magnitude. I look at my mother questioningly.

"Who's that?"

"That's Annie Dinkles."

Annie Dinkles! The orphan girl who I was sure would look as lame as her name, and here she is, no country bumpkin, but a luminous beauty

"She was Annie Cohen then," Mom went on, "and this was taken when she was living with us."

"I thought she lived with ChaRussa," I said.

"Well …" Mom hesitates. "My heart breaks when I think of her," she goes on, and Annie's story unfolds. In contrast to Benny's tragic aquatic end or the daring escapades of Gentleman Jim and Davy, Annie's destiny was hauntingly romantic, almost operatic, an aria befitting her great beauty.

While living with Grandpa's sister, Tante ChaRussa, she fell for a man who, my mother said, was as handsome as Annie was beautiful, and he proposed. "They were young and in love," Mom said, "and so well-mated, the kind of couple you enjoyed seeing together. When they looked at each other you could hear wedding bells."

Tante ChaRussa thought otherwise. By all accounts, ChaRussa was a wonderful gal, warm and caring with a quick smile and a smart wit, and just about my grandmother's best friend. But she was a woman of her time. In ChaRussa's world, there were no options as to appropriate behavior where courtship and marriage were concerned. In the name of misguided propriety, she lowered the boom on Annie with a common dictate of the day: "You cannot marry till my oldest daughter marries!"

Blinded by love and trapped by tradition, Annie ran out into a stormy night. Through the rain swept streets of Brooklyn she ran, right to my grandparents' door. Grandpa took her in and ChaRussa stopped talking to him. "What was I to do?" he said. "Leave her standing out there alone in the rain?"

For reasons lost in time, Annie's fiancée soon disappeared, and someone "made a match" for her with the curiously named Izzy Dinkles.

She went on to become Mrs. Dinkles, and I wonder if she carried with her the memory of her lost beau. I wonder if she became one of the zillions walking around with secret holes in their secret hearts.

The thing of it is that she and Aunt Betty were both getting ready to marry at the same time, under my grandparents' roof. The irony of it was not lost on me.

Annie and Betty were the same age. They had started out together sharing girlhood secrets on the front steps and in the rear parlor of the house in London where they both lived. Now, twenty years later, in a magic show staged by fire and fate, they were brides-to-be living together in the same apartment in Brooklyn.

While I ponder Annie's melancholy entry into womanhood, my mother and I rifle through a slew of other photos taken mostly in the 1920s. Here are unknown friends and relatives posed, as had been Annie, in theatrical artifices favored by photographers of the day. We see a plain woman looking pensively out of a phony castle window; children of immigrants all done up in implausibly upper-crust togs; and working-class couples holding hands in front of regal, often floral, backdrops. Then comes the boy.

A lad of five or six, dressed in a Little Lord Fauntleroy outfit, he is captured in a very early studio portrait with all the fancy flourishes of the day. From leafy foliage on a plant stand to a draped curtain, this is a picture of refinement, almost literary in its references. The boy looks directly into the camera, facing the world with cocky optimism. I look at my mother, quizzically.

"Gentleman Jim," she said. "In England, before it all happened."

Gentleman Jim! In England! He and his brother Davy and my Uncle Jack must have been the closest of boyhood friends. Chasing each other cross Stepney Green; exploring alleys and side streets; or playing hide-and-seek on the sly in the cooperage in the rear, out there among the kegs. That is when they weren't posing for pictures to be sent to America.

I gaze at the tintype, peering right into the eyes of that little lad. A dainty fellow he is, prissy in his velveteen suit and long curls, for God's sake, and with the same fine porcelain features as his sister Annie. I look at the picture for a long time. How could such a boy, pretty, privileged, and full of promise, how could such a boy end up a vagabond poet, the black sheep of our family, slipping and sliding on the shores—or the rails—of life?

"Who knows what went on in that orphanage," my mother says. "Who knows how it was in there, way back then. How it damaged them, before they came to live with us. He was the most sensitive, I think. Who knows what effect it had on him."

I look at the photos. Annie. Beautiful, star-crossed Annie. Joseph. Proud and sure and young and ready for life. Joseph before he became Gentleman Jim. What happened to them? Life, I suspect. Life closed in on them, like a thief in the night, and stole what lay before them, just as it had done to Grandma and Grandpa.

And then of course Goldie appears, immortalized in sepia, smiling wistfully at the camera as if tomorrow were hers, a little girl of three with a halo of soft yellow hair. Hair as golden as the little band that bordered her dress of taffeta, starchy yet silky material brought to England from India, Grandma had said. A little girl who loved to dance. A golden girl, Grandpa had called her; the light within their home, he had said. She was the lively one, and wherever Grandpa was within the house, he knew where Goldie danced. He could hear the taffeta of her little dress, how it rustled as she moved, how it crackled and whispered: *I am happy, Papa. I am dancing.*

An unspoken bond existed between Goldie and me. They had called her Golden Girl. They had called me Golden Boy. I doubt anyone knew as much about her as I did, except for Aunt Betty and Uncle Jack, who said very little. On two separate trips to London, I set out to find her grave to let her know that someone still cared.

On the first trip in the 1970s, neither the cemetery where Yetta was buried nor an unexpected jaunt through a London children's cemetery bore results.

On the second trip, both contact with the Federation of Jewish Synagogues and a determined hunt for a Sephardic Cemetery yield dust.

Goldie had to be buried somewhere, but she seemed to be nowhere.

• • •

42

DISCOVERY

B itter is the day, a typical London day in late November, a day colored gray. On such a day did the parlor walls at 45 Redmans Road turn black, scorched by burnt taffeta, sad proof that fire and smoke had robbed Goldie Cohen of her brief life, charring the leaves on our family tree, and causing it to wither much too soon.

Five days later, at the dawn of December, on the threshold of winter, her remains would be buried, deep down in the damp earth of 1908 London. What a dismal goodbye to "a gay, lively child who loved to dance," and whose last steps—possibly merry and certainly doomed—would shape our family's fate.

On a future gray white London day, precisely 105 years later, I have come to say *hello, how has it gone?* to the little girl my grandparents lost and the unrealized woman the rest of us would never know.

Her mother/my grandmother had thought of her every day since, she had said. Yet for the most part Goldie had receded into memory, as people do, only to live on in the land of family legend where, by definition, visit is outlawed.

No one knows where Goldie sleeps, and no one has even tried to visit her since the day she was laid to rest more than a lifetime ago. It has taken me twenty-five years to find her, and now I come, bearer of unexpected greeting on a voyage that exceeds explanation and that, I am convinced, is no random act.

At East Ham in the far end of the East End of London, you will find High Street North. Armed with a Journey Planner printout fresh off my hotel computer, I emerge from the nearest tube stop, only three stops past Stepney Green where once my grandparents lived and prospered, and where Goldie danced. Mercifully the station opens onto the High Street, a long, long thoroughfare lined with apparently Arab owned or managed shops and stores, cafes and eateries, public service buildings, small businesses... and one very old, easily unnoticed Jewish burial ground, or so the Journey Planner printout says. Even as I walk rain starts to fall.

These days Plashet Cemetery is locked. However, the Federation of London Synagogues has kindly provided access, and I am set to meet someone who will open the gates and show me the way to Goldie's place. Having learned that maps and directions often do not accord with actual geography, I allow myself plenty of time to walk and wander, to look and to see, to explore and, most probably, lose my way.

How still is High Street this morning, not what you'd expect with all those shops and dining spots, an odd quiet due no doubt to gloom and rain and early hour. Yet the absence of foot and car traffic allows the worn charms of the street to surface, uninterrupted. Brick buildings extend as far as the eye can see, jammed together yet picturesque in the 19th century row house fashion. Stacks of chimneys, lined up in crisp columns of three or four, aim upward in unison like artillery targeting grey skies above.

Plashet Cemetery, according to my map, should be a stone's throw from Plashet Park. This means detouring past the park, actually called Plashet Grove. I am a few blocks past the grove, larger in reality than on the map, when instinct tells me that I am walking in the wrong direction. A kind stranger guides me to where I ought to be, which is where I started out from, back on High Street North.

For the most part, High Street curves its way through the heart of a working-class neighborhood. Keeping an eye out for the cemetery, it occurs to me that the face of this street has not changed much since that fateful day which stained our family calendar in 1908. Neither, I am sure, has the weather. The sky is pewter. The air is damp. A mist falls softly on the silent street.

For a moment, I think I hear the snort of a horse and the screech of wheels, wooden wheels grinding slowly against cobblestone, a shrill noise followed by the soothing clip clop of horses hooves. A dark carriage clatters by. In its wake men in formal hats and tweed overcoats walk slowly, heads bowed. Women pull fur-trimmed coats about them to ward off the chill, and I can see them sniffle into lace hankies.

Sunlight streams down from behind a cloud. In its fiery path, both horse and carriage vaporize, and the street wakens to new life. But these men and women who scurry by me on this blustery day wear parka and ski cap, not fur and fedora. Gone too are the warm wood and earthy whinny of horse and carriage. In their stead there are only engine's growls, bitter fumes, and the glittery flash of chrome-and-steel automobile. Time is a thief.

Time, it appears, is also a magician. Somehow the Russian teahouses that lined this street a generation ago have turned into Muslim vegetarian restaurants. Surnames on street signs and mailboxes that once evoked cobbled villages of Eastern Europe now stir visions of a veiled and honeyed Araby. Signs in cafes and butcher shops that once read *Kosher*, meaning foodstuffs fit to eat under Jewish religious law, today read *Halal*, for the same under Muslim belief.

Time is forever, and architecture is proof. As I walk down High Street, houses devoid of color and ornamentation unfold before me, each connected to the other in a tidy unvarnished parade of no-nonsense style and structure. Made of stone and brick these houses seem to say *I am here for good,* no matter the changing ethnicity of this corner of London or the state of the world at large.

I pass by slowly, wondering when Plashet Cemetery will appear, certain that gates of iron will rise before me suddenly; tremendous gates, to be sure, dark in color and fearsome to the eye, as vast and indestructible as eternity.

Taking in the side streets, I gaze at more dusty row houses, linked to each other in timeless comfort. Modest homes these are, fronted by gardens the size of postage stamps, barren and waiting for spring.

Paned windows beckon. I try to see inside these windows of the houses passing by, these same windowpanes that once looked out upon my grandparents when they walked by, fine and young and proud, with our family that came before. I try to see within, but sunshine and shadow and curtain and shutter cloud my view. Yet these windows and adjacent doorways, these portals to the past, look back fondly and not in silence. *Welcome,* say the doorways. *We know,* say the windows. *We were there then. We have seen. We have heard.*

I have looked too much and daydreamed too deeply. Based on the street number, I have obviously bypassed Plashet Cemetery. Icy wind whips the air. Taking refuge, I dart into a café that could just as well have been on a main street in Calcutta. After scented hot tea and an unidentifiable, delectably fruity, and satisfying pastry, I brace myself and walk out onto the chilly street again.

Neither gloved hand nor long scarf nor wool pea coat can warm me, even as the sun shines and more than one passerby nods in cozy silent greeting. Yet the chill I feel has nothing to do with raw weather.

On the plane coming over, I had been overcome by the enormity of this visit, a feeling I could not quite define. Perhaps it is simply that the skewered ingredients of my childhood, events unexpected and beyond anyone's control, placed me firmly in my grandparents' world—in their time, to these streets that they knew, to a graveyard they came to call upon long before they ever expected to.

Ironically, Plashet Cemetery is only a few short blocks from the East Ham tube stop from where I first entered the street. There is no dramatic access here, only a fencing of iron spires, greenish with age and inset with decorative crests.

Brick columns flank Plashet's entry, separating it from an imperious adjacent building. The left column, a weathered testament to time, retains its original pinkish color. Its mate, however, is painted half-white and ground to top. My eye follows the white strip to a nameplate right out of the Arabian Nights, evident owner of the great house next door. A collar of stone trims the top of the whitewashed pillar. Chiseled into its well-worn face is one telling, startlingly passé phrase: *Jews Cemetery.*

"Mr. Gorney!" the voice belongs to the caretaker, who approaches the gate from within. With a smile as bright and cheery as his greeting, he unlocks the gate.

Plashet is small in size, not much wider than the span of its entry. A desolate tree looks down upon rows of gravestones in appropriately serene order. For the most part these are simple and weatherworn.

"Your grandparents?" the caretaker asks as we walk.

"No," I say telling him why I have come, Goldie's story, and as I speak, I wonder what her place will look like. What pains did my grandparents take to see that Goldie would be forever remembered?

No doubt it is a small gravestone, a little stone for a little girl.

Well, no matter how humble the monument, just to see her name inscribed in granite will be enough. Just to place a pebble or rock upon her tombstone, a time-honored token of remembrance, will suffice. What a meaningful tradition, a way of saying someone still cares, someone has come a long way to bring warm wishes, to say I love you from Mama and Papa, even after all these years … that in itself will be reward enough.

As we approach the site, I begin to understand feelings that had evaded definition earlier. How fitting that I, brought up my grandparents at a time when they ought not to be raising children, loved and taught and shaped by them, old and old-fashioned as they were, how fitting it is that I should be the one to come here, to bring warm welcome to their little girl gone.

It is more than even that. They had sailed away from these shores, this Britain that they loved, hearts seared by unseen fire, souls scarred by unspeakable catastrophe. They had set out to reinvent themselves, if it were possible, to seek comfort in a new life in a new country an ocean away. Now I return, traveler on a journey they dared not imagine a lifetime ago. And the thing of it is this. No one has come here, where Goldie sleeps, no one has been here since she was lowered into this ground, this British earth, in 1908.

The caretaker double-checks the location of Goldie's grave. It is a short walk to where she rests, he says, and we proceed past graves, ornate and simple, stone homes of dead Jews with names resonant of Old London and the world they knew. *Tobias. Louisa, Zachariah and Adelaide. And Nell.* Paging Charles Dickens is all I can think. But other more telling thoughts take root on that short walk.

I have come I am certain as an emissary on behalf of my grandparents. Informed by a sense of duty, hesitation fills my every step. Gravel snaps underneath our feet as we walk, the caretaker and I. Crunch. Crackle. A starchy hiss and a sputter. Not unlike the sound of stiff material swishing when women in taffeta walked or a little girl danced.

"We're here," says the caretaker.

We stare at Goldie's grave in disbelief.

"Look," he continues, pointing to the ground. "There's nothing."

He is right. There is nothing. Nothing. No name. No headstone. No gravestone. No marker. Nothing. Nothing but a small bed framed by wood and topped by pebbles and rocks. Makeshift and austere in the extreme.

I am speechless.

Then I notice something even more baffling. Goldie has company. Right near her little plot lay three or four like graves also topped by pebbles. Based on size each holds a child, each of whom shares a predicament in common with our Goldie. None have markers. I ask the caretaker about this but he has no explanation.

My gaze wanders to several rows of plain headstones nearby. "That's where the paupers are buried," says the caretaker. "They say they don't have money for a funeral but they manage to put up a stone."

We look back again at Goldie's grave. The caretaker puts his hand to his chin and speaks slowly as if thinking out loud.

"Is it because Jews wait a year before putting up a tombstone?"

"I had never thought of that. In a year's time, my grandparents were in America. I bet that's it."

• • •

But that is not it at all. Future research dispels any such connection.

First, the Federation of London Synagogues advises, "while waiting about 11/12 months to erect/consecrate a tombstone is common custom in both England and America, there is no Jewish law that prescribes such a time period. Tombstones are erected much sooner for burials taking place in Israel."

Secondly, Plaza Jewish Community Chapel in New York City believes that in America the custom of waiting a year before putting up a stone may be due to the complexities of creating a monument, which can often take about a year.

In short the theory of waiting a year has no religious precedent and does not explain the lack of a tombstone for Goldie and the other children buried near her.

Furthermore, every Internet site I view explicitly states that Jewish tradition requires mourners to mark the grave of the deceased and that placement of a headstone signifies respect even as it allows and encourages visit. The question that aches to be answered can be expressed in one undying word – why?

Why would any grieving Jewish parent defy sensible ritual and bury a departed child without honoring his or her brief existence on this earth? What conceivable reasoning could have given birth to this little colony of lifeless children without names?

Perhaps, a friend suggests, answers can be found in obscure religious practice or long forgotten local custom. Who better to know what might have happened all those years ago in England than the Federation of London Synagogues. My first e-mail of inquiry goes astray. However, subsequent correspondence garners response that is as enlightening as it is chilling.

> Many years go when a child or baby was buried at our cemeteries the burial took place in a grave already occupied by an adult. On many occasions there was no tombstone for the adult and no tombstone for the child/baby. Some of the adult graves have had tombstones erected and there is normally no mention of the child/baby that is buried in the same grave. It appears to have been the custom at the time, all those years ago, that the burial was something that was not spoken about even with other family members, and with most cases the family did not know where the burial took place, only that the child/baby had been buried.

Customs of course have changed, and the Federation goes on to explain that "when dealing with a similar situation nowadays the parents/family attend the burial and know where it has taken place and have the option of erecting a memorial stone ..."

> We believe that it was just the custom at the time with all the Jewish burial societies dealing with children/babies. We are unable to comment on the procedure adopted by the non-Jewish cemeteries many years ago.

So much for my notion that High Street North bore sad witness to Goldie's funeral procession so many years ago. More than likely the doors and windows of its houses looked out upon a solitary wagon rolling down the street.

Just as likely Goldie had entered the gates of Plashet Cemetery alone. And when she was lowered into that cold soil on the brink of a London winter all those years ago there was no one to watch over her. No one pondered the freshly shoveled earth above her grave. No one said a prayer. No one whispered goodbye.

Everybody who had loved her—her parents/my grandparents, her older brother/my Uncle Jack, her big sister/my Aunt Betty—had moved away. In a new land they would start new lives, separated from Goldie by an ocean of water and a sea of tears.

• • •

I had traveled light years from the world Goldie knew. I had come all this way, transcending time and place to pay tribute to her. Standing at her unfinished gravesite, so shockingly overlooked, I begin to wonder: Why? Why would I search so long and so hard simply to find out where she was buried or to try to uncover the truth about how she died? Or, for that matter, travel half-a-continent away to far-off Romania to try to find relatives whose names I do not even know.

Perhaps it is the writer in me, seeking forgotten stories worthy of salvage and retelling. Or maybe I had come to London and gone to Romania for the self same reasons that inspire every genealogical hunt, everyone who looks deeply into his or her past: the need to find out more about our earlier families. Most of all, the hope of finding a piece of oneself in those who came before. A little bit of all of it comes into play, I am sure, but as I stand at Goldie's grave I realize that something greater is at work.

Sunshine warms the stones and pebbles that blanket Goldie. Wind whistles through the branches of that wretchedly barren tree that oversees this colony of the dead. A melancholy sound it is that informs Goldie's rest, at odds with the music of her life, taffeta rustling as she sashayed gaily across a gaslit parlor to the delight of her father/my grandfather.

And this is the thing of it: there exists an unspoken bond between us. No one could have loved Goldie more than my grandparents. No one could have loved me more than my grandparents.

It is as if everything—from my parents' ruinous marriage to my father's insistent absence to my grandparents' long years and generous hearts—all that coalesced to make me who I am, that made them the most important people in my life, that all of it brought me here. I was more than a messenger, come on behalf of my grandparents. I was here to honor the little girl whose unexpected death changed everything, who in one fiery, tragic, possibly foolish moment forged our family's future.

Stories are the spur. It was the warm magic of my grandmother's bedtime tales that propelled me to find Romania, half-a-world away, and the splendid oratory of my grandfather's tableside talks that sent me back in time, placing my feet firmly on the pavements of Edwardian London. Without intent, my grandparents had gifted me with the keys to the family kingdom, made me the keeper of the stories, and molded me into the family archivist. But there is yet another side to it.

Mine is a mission born of the need to become whole and to survive well, as instinctive and primal as animals huddling together for warmth under the chilly yoke of a glacial winter, the same solitary need that has spurred every young man or woman to dare leave home to find his or her self.

Growing up in my grandparents' house, I was a boy apart, brought up by ancients, moored in another time and from another place. I was the boy whose name was hyphenated on the nameplates in the foyer of the small apartment house where I grew up, my name tacked onto that of my grandparents on the mailbox of an apartment for which my aunt and uncle paid the rent, proof of a family splintered and undone.

That is what fuels these journeys, makes me embark on these adventures, compels me to explore the world of these vanished Londoners, at once prosperous and tragic, and to look for these lost Romanians, these forgotten people who populate the places of the past... our past.

Standing at Goldie's grave, weathered and shockingly forgotten as it is, I understand why it is so important to travel, to find, to be here. Redmans Road. Mile End. Plashet Cemetery. Piccadilly Circus. Iasi. Moldavia. Stefanesti. Being there transforms these places from realms of memory and myth to here and now. In these places where once we walked the stories become real.

What drives me to explore the past? Not only the writer in me. No, mine is a mission that exceeds curiosity, that is more than adventurous or merely romantic. Goldie and our London that might have been. Haim and Roza, lost in distant, troubled Romania, as well as Monis and his mystery family. These are the people who dwell within my ancestral house. That is where they live. Theirs are the nameplates in the foyer there. What drives me to search for them, even though they have been gone for so long? Why is it vital that I find out who they were, where they lived, and how it went with them? The answer is as simple as looking in the mirror.

I come from a broken home. I want to put the pieces together. I want to make the family whole.

• • •

EPILOGUE

"**I** was thirteen years old when they sent me to apprentice with my uncle." The voice belongs to Grandpa. "He was a mean one. Every morning he would kick me out of bed, and he would shout: 'Get up, get out of bed, get going you lazy loafer! The beggar is already at the tenth village.'"

It was a story Grandpa told often, and he never missed a beat or an inflection. With the instinctive smarts of a born storyteller, he managed, with splendid economy, to transport the listener to a lost world he had once known.

After my grandfather was gone, I took it upon myself to tell his story to anyone who would listen. I could not equal the rich tone of his voice or the look in his eye. But in taking charge of his story, I learned something about the teller and the tale and the delicate ties that bind fact and fancy, reality and perception.

Time picks the pockets of truth, and genealogical research demands restitution. Paperwork and pictures serve as guardians of proof. Birth and death certificates reveal precisely when and where and how our ancestors came into and left this life. Ship records chart their earthly comings and goings, departures and arrivals, narrow escapes, and safe landings.

Photos are pieces of time preserved. Each picture captures a moment in the lives of those who have preceded us, showing how they looked and carried themselves, what they wore, and where they lived and loved, and thrived or failed. Words and pictures not only rectify skewered realities and quirks of memory, but may unlock doors to a dimly lit past. This is the backbone, the hard evidence, of genealogy.

Despite some cherished finds, "hard evidence" largely evaded my genealogical world. I had found Goldie's grave in England, but could not find the graves of my great-grandparents or other relatives in Romania. Too many photos have been lost. Too many archives are hard to access. Too much paperwork has been discarded or remains unknown. Letters, especially from the Old Country, would have been rich sources of names, places, and specifics of life, often divulged in idle news or gossip. With minor exception, no one in our family thought to save such personal papers.

Other more complex obstacles arise. Mine is a research foiled by sheer accidents of geography and history. My Romanians lived and died in a world driven mad by unprecedented war. Here bombs fall not on battlefields, but on places where people live and firestorms incinerate records. Here men, women, and children are torn from their homes, displaced, scattered to the winds. Here, finally, marching armies massacre and loot, defacing cemeteries, smashing tombstones, and reducing entire villages to ash.

My lost family lived in a Europe reshaped for a while into a refugee continent, a war-torn, bloodstained arena of people in flight, running for their lives, taking desperate shelter when they could in attics and cellars, forest and hayloft, behind locked doors and between fake walls. To be caught is to be transported to a per-verse madman's hell - shocking places dedicated to the destruction of the human spirit and to death by unspeakable means. When it is all over, and the dust of that terrible Holocaust settles, an anxious peace sets up further, unexpected obstacles.

Had they survived, my relatives would have known further sadness, at once trapped behind an Iron Curtain, frozen in a Cold War, and petrified by ruthless repression, one tyranny replacing another. In the end, shackled nations would fight for and gain freedom, finding a new future. For genealogists, locked vaults would open, allowing the past to invite inspection. Yet for all the newfound opportunity, an unexpected and profound barrier thwarts my research: Romania does not micro-film its archives.

Nowhere is this lack more acute than in searching for the elusive Monis Grisariu. Without diary or document, finding out where my great-uncle lived, what he did with his life, and how it ended proves futile. Without so much as a simple mention of his wife and children, identifying them is like looking for a needle in a very old and brittle haystack, no less finding out what fortunes or misfortunes fate held in store for them.

My family's past seems destined to remain mired in anonymity. Relatives with photos from Romania, friends, and neighbors who could have been sources of information are long gone. All of it happened so many years ago, how would I ever find anyone who knew the Grisarius of Iasi or Stefanesti? Or the Cohen Brothers in London?

There is, I would learn, another route to the past, compelling and invisible. Devoid of photographic image or printer's ink, it would present itself to me in several guises: in my grandmother's bedtime stories, through the oft-told telling of my grandfather's apprentice days, in the belated reminiscences of my father's oldest brother, Uncle Jerry, and in a second look at the late lives of four orphaned cousins from London. It is a route so delicate that a mere whisper can light the way, a soft laugh or sigh bring back the departed, and a shift in tone lift rusted anchors of memory.

I can see my grandmother at the kitchen table, leaning forward, her voice low in that special register reserved for choice words from Europe. I can hear her now: "Like we used to say in the Old Country, you can survive a smack, but words last forever."

Words last forever, and take on a life of their own, especially in stories passed on from generation to generation. New narrators may embroider the truth or add commentary. Yet in the end it is the word, no matter how altered or glorified, that inspires investigation, enlightens the mind, and can even transform the heart.

Some words, some stories, are at risk of loss, victims of incident and condition. Through a fluke of circumstance, I meet a first cousin on my father's side, Niche Gorney, daughter of Jerry, my father's oldest brother. "You need to meet my father," Niche says. "You look like him and you sound like him."

I never did meet Jerry Gorney. Time was not on our side, but I did have the privilege of speaking to him. He was just over 100 years old, living in Montreal, and he was sharp as ever.

"You come from a very old family in Poland, three generations of writers and public speakers."

When the Gorneys emigrated, they left Jerry, oldest of the boys, behind with the grandparents. Because he was the only one, they were able to send him to university. He was a creative man who became an actor in Poland, and a writer, and he had an interest in photography.

We have a shared heritage of creativity, Uncle Jerry and me. I know this from his voice that is my voice, from his memories of Poland and my father's family over there and how well he tells his story of coming to America in the 1930s, mercifully before Hitler, on the waves of the worldwide Depression.

No matter the paucity of evidence or lack of printed word and picture, I am heir to a legacy of genealogical plenty. Mine is a birthright of remarkable stories told by great storytellers: Grandpa, Grandma, Cousin Helen, Uncle Jack, Aunt Rae and Uncle Mauritz, and now Uncle Jerry—each in his or her own voice, each moored to a specific time and place, or places, all celebrating our communal past.

Family fables have powers that exceed reality. Driven by very old magic, these are stories that come from places deep within our fathers and mothers, and grandfathers and grandmothers, aunts and uncles, and cousins close and distant. All had heard the same stories at the knees of their own fathers and mothers, grandparents, aunts and uncles and cousins, all of whom had heard the very same stories from yet others who came before. These are our earlier selves, and their stories are our stories, tales told in voices that echo through the ages till they seep into our hearts and begin to murmur in our souls.

These are the voices of our very being; voices first heard by ancient ancestors huddled around an open fire in the dark, under a starlit ceremonial canopy or a stone arch, or at a child's bedtime by fireside, by gaslight, by naked bulb, and halogen lamp.

These are the voices of the ages. Voices spit out of a record player to fill a silent room, or floating on the air at the twist of a radio knob. Voices emerging out of the past on tape, on disc, on mp3. Voices that summon lost moments in word and with a sudden breath whisk us into misty realms where deceased, unknown, or forgotten ancestors dwell.

These are the same voices that once whispered in the deep of night while wolves howled at the moon or, even now, glide in on wings of dawn, barely heard in the silken sighs of dreams gone by morning light.

On some fragile level, the voices of these vanished relatives are always with us by dint of who they were, where they lived, what they dreamed and achieved, or not. Their existences, the adventures of their lives, are stitched into the fabric of their stories. Their time on Earth is woven into the cloth of which we are made, a genetic tapestry that wallpapers our perpetual family room. Exceeding time and space, it wraps around us, infusing our cells with a history of the heart. Sometimes unspoken, often unseen, it binds us instinctively and invisibly to those who came before.

Their stories are the glue that holds us together, the raw material of our DNA, the very stuff of our lives. In their realities lay pools of ageless insight and springs of healing warmth.

Listen. Their voices call to us from other rooms and other places. Strain hard to hear. Covered in dust and muted by time, they whisper of where once we came, who we were, and who we are…and what we might become.

Listen. How gently their words steer and counsel, how silently they teach. Pay heed and you will uncover messages buried in the telling of their tales, lessons at once vibrant and current yet often overlooked.

It is a simple truth: families are everlasting and those who are gone never die. Their presence resonates in the eternal plasma of stories, the lifeblood that sustains us, connecting generation to generation. Look. At the pictures. In the mirror. Listen to those who came before us. Let their stories guide and advise, shaping the present through the lessons of the past. The thing of it is that the past is always present. Listen...

• • •

RECIPES

BROILED SAUSAGES
Karnatzlach

Little grilled garlic-stuffed sausages

Uncle Mauritz made these zesty little sausages at home, but in Jewish Romanian restaurants on New York's Lower East Side karnatzlach seemed to have increased considerably in size. By all accounts, these were originally on the smaller side. They are also a flavor crossbreed, drawn from both Moldavian Breaded Meat Patties and Mititei (homemade charcoal-broiled little sausages usually grilled outdoors). Even its name is a culinary cross between the Romanian *carnati*, for sausages, and the Yiddish suffix ("lach") for little.

Serves 6 (2 sausages per serving)
1-½ lb. medium lean ground beef or lamb
1 medium onion, grated
1 carrot, peeled and grated
1 large garlic clove, crushed
3 tbsp. fresh parsley, chopped
1 tbsp. sage
½ tsp. fresh ground black pepper
1 tsp. hot Hungarian paprika
½ tsp. crushed red pepper
1 egg, slightly beaten flour for dredging

1. Put all ingredients in a bowl, except for the flour. Mix well, first with a wooden spoon and then with your hands, until completely blended.

2. Using a tablespoon, shape the meat mixture into sausages about 3 inches x 1 inch wide. Narrow the ends so that the patties look like little cigars, and lightly coat with flour. You should have about a dozen sausages.

3. Preheat your broiler or grill to medium. Broil sausages, turning until thoroughly browned on all sides, about 10-12 minutes.

Serve hot or cold. Add either mustard or sautéed-browned onions. Goes well with mamaliga!

CORNMEAL POLENTA
Mamaliga

Polenta, Romanian style.

Naturally golden and divinely fluffy, mamaliga is Romania's national comfort food, fabled in song and story, eaten morning, noon and night, and with various regional fixings.

Serves 6
Prep time 15 mins. Cook time 15 mins
3 cups water
2 tsp salt
2 tbsp butter
1-½ cups yellow corn meal, coarse or medium ground

1. Heat water over high flame in a pot or kettle. Bring to a roaring boil.

2. Sprinkle a scant tbsp of cornmeal into the boiling water. When water resumes boiling, add the remainder of the cornmeal all at once. Stir constantly with a stick or the long end of a wooden spoon.

3. Once cornmeal begins bubbling, turn heat down. Continue to stir until the mamaliga thickens and starts to pull away from the pot. Be careful to avoid boiling cornmeal, which should spit out of the pot as the mixture cooks.

4. Keep stirring, in one direction only, and over low heat. Expect the mixture to clump as you stir.

5. Mamaliga should be ready in about 10-15 minutes. To test if it is finished, wet the end of a wooden spoon with cold water and place it straight up in the cornmeal mixture. Twist spoon two or three times, then remove. If the spoon is clean the mamaliga is done.

6. Shake the pot and immediately turn it upside down onto a wooden board. Your mamaliga should retain the shape of the pot. Serve immediately while hot.

In the region that my grandmother came from it was customary to slice the mamaliga into portions using a string or cord and to serve it with Bryndza (sheep cheese).

Mamaliga may be eaten with cheese or sour cream. Or it can be served as a side dish with meat, fish, or eggs or red peppers.

EGGPLANT DIP

Putlagela Vinete Tocate

In the Old Country, my grandmother said, they roasted the eggplant for putlagela over an open flame until the skin charred and its smoky essence permeated the pulp. In America, she baked it in the oven.

1 large eggplant
1 med onion, grated
1 tsp lemon juice
½ cup olive oil
salt and pepper to taste
wooden spoon

1. Choose a good-size eggplant and one that is firm and smooth. Broil or roast it over a top burner flame, turning constantly until tender.

2. When the skin is seared, let eggplant cool slightly. Dip your fingers in cold water and peel eggplant skin until pulp is totally visible. While still warm, place the pulp on a wooden board and begin to mash it with a wooden knife (or the edge of any wood utensil and board). Add a couple of drops of olive oil as you mash and chop. Use wooden utensils only or the pulp will darken and turn bitter.

3. Transfer the paste to a wooden bowl, still using a wooden spoon. Stir constantly with the spoon, adding about ½ cup of the olive oil or, to taste, drop by drop. Now add lemon juice, drop-by-drop, and salt and pepper, also to taste. Keep stirring until the seeds dissolve and the paste is firm yet smooth. The eggplant blend should double in size and turn pale green.

Store in a cool, dry place. Grate some raw onion over it just before serving. You may also add parsley, green pepper, red pepper, or pine nuts. Garnish with ripe black olives. Serve on wheat crackers or pita bread.

TURKISH COFFEE
Cafea Turkeasca

In our family making foamy fragrant Turkish coffee was Uncle Mauritz's specialty. To make a good Turkish coffee you need the right bean, he advised. He said that the best coffee bean to use is pure mocha. If mocha is unavailable you may use continental or espresso beans. Any bean used must be ground for Turkish coffee.

It is important also to use the right coffee pot. The traditional pot is called an ibrik and it has a long narrow spout. The ibrik can be purchased inexpensively at Turkish, Greek, or Middle Eastern food shops. If you don't have an ibrik, a simple pot will work

Serves 2
Preparation time: minimal. Brew time: 10 mins.
2 Turkish coffee (or demitasse) cups cold water
2 lumps sugar
2 heaping tsp coffee

1. Place water, sugar, and coffee in ibrik. Do not stir. Set on medium-high heat..

2. Add sugar. Warm the water until sugar disslves. Stir coffee several times with a long spoon and then lower heat. Coffee will rise quickly to the pot brim and foam will coat the top. Do not let coffee boil.

3. Remove pot from heat and skim off foam. Place pot back over heat. Warm until coffee rises again to the rim. Take care not to boil. Remove from heat again and skim foam. Repeat this process three times. Just after coffee rises the last time, dribble a drop or two of cold water into pot so grounds settle to the bottom.

Pour the coffee into cups. You should have two cups of foamy coffee.